JUNIOR
READING EXPERT

A Theme-Based Reading Course for Young EFL Learners

Level **3**

JUNIOR
READING EXPERT

Level 3

Series Editor   Ji-hyun Kim
Project Editors   Eun-kyung Kim, Jun-hee Kim, Yoon-joung Choi
Contributing Writers   Curtis Thompson, Bryce Olk, Angela Hai Yue Lan, Patrick Ferraro, MyAn Le, Keeran Murphy
Illustrators   Soo-hyeon Lee, Yoon-seo Jung
Design   Hoon-jung Ahn, Ji-young Ki
Editorial Designer   Sun-hee Kim

ISBN   979-11-253-4042-3 53740
Photo Credits   www.shutterstock.com

3rd Edition
Copyright ⓒ 2023 NE Neungyule, Inc.
First Printing 5 January 2023
7th Printing 15 September 2024

INTRODUCTION

Junior Reading Expert is a four-level reading course for EFL readers, with special relevance for older elementary school students and junior high school students. Students will acquire not only reading skills but also knowledge of various contemporary and academic topics.

Features

Covers Dynamic, Contemporary Topics

Engaging topics, including culture, sports, and literature, are developed in an easy and interesting way to motivate students.

Expands Knowledge

Each unit is composed of two closely related readings under one topic heading. These readings allow students to explore the theme in depth.

Features Longer Passages

EFL students are seldom exposed to long reading passages and therefore tend to find them difficult. Compelling and well-developed passages designed specifically for EFL students will help them learn to handle longer passages with ease.

Presents Different Text Types of Passages

Reading passages are presented as articles, letters, debates, interviews, and novels. This helps students become familiarized with a variety of writing formats and styles through different genres of readings.

Provides Various Exercises for Reading Skills

All readings are accompanied by different types of tasks, such as multiple choice, matching, short answer, true/false, and fill-in-the-blank. These exercises are carefully designed to develop the following reading skills: understanding main ideas, identifying details, drawing inferences, and recognizing organizational structures.

Series Overview

Each level of *Junior Reading Expert* is composed of 20 units, with two related readings accompanying each unit. The number of words in each Reading 1 passage is as follows:

Level 1: 150–170 words
Level 2: 170–190 words
Level 3: 190–210 words
Level 4: 210–230 words

Format

Reading 1

Reading 1 takes students into the first of the unit's two readings. Being the main reading of the unit, Reading 1 deals with various interesting and important topics in great depth. The passages gradually increase in difficulty as students progress through the book.

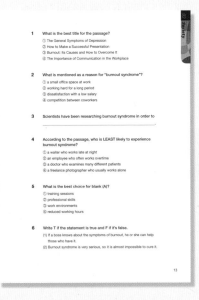

Different Types of Questions

A full page of different types of questions follows Reading 1. The questions concentrate on important reading skills, such as understanding the main idea, identifying details, drawing inferences, and recognizing the organizational structure.

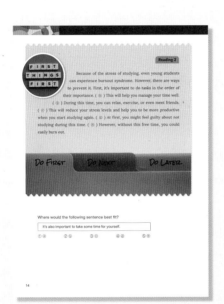

Reading 2

Reading 2 offers a second reading passage on the unit topic, the length of which is from 90 to 110 words. Reading 2 supplements Reading 1 with additional information, further explanation, or a new point of view.

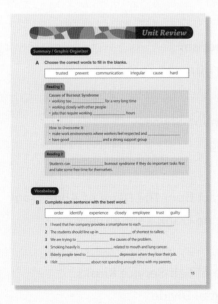

Unit Review

A Summary / Graphic Organizer
Either a summary or a graphic organizer is provided for Reading 1 and Reading 2 to facilitate a better understanding of the flow of passages. Performing this task also encourages the development of systematic comprehension skills.

B Vocabulary
Each unit is concluded with vocabulary practice. It checks students' knowledge of essential vocabulary words. Vocabulary practice requires students to either match definitions or choose words in context.

Table of Contents

Reading 1

One morning, the Prime Minister of India was seen picking up trash during a walk by the beach. Later, he posted about it on social media with the words "Plogging at the beach. It lasted for over 30 minutes." But what is "plogging"?

"Plogging" is made up of the English word "jogging" and the Swedish phrase *plocka upp*, meaning "pick up." ⓐ It is the act of picking up trash while jogging or walking fast. ⓑ So a trash bag is a necessary item for people in Sweden. ⓒ It began in Sweden in 2016, when Erik Ahlström noticed trash on the streets on his way to work. ⓓ He picked up the trash, and this became a habit. Over time, he even did it on his daily runs! As more and more people saw Ahlström's actions, the movement spread across Sweden.

Now, plogging is a global movement, as people talk about it online and offline. A quick search for "#plogging" on social media will give you thousands of pictures of people _____(A)_____.
It's easy to see why the movement is growing, as anyone can easily go out and pick up some trash. So why don't you give it a try yourself?

1 What is the best title for the passage?

① Build a Daily Routine for Your Health

② Why Streets in Sweden Are So Clean

③ Is Social Media Useful for Environmental Issues?

④ A Popular and Meaningful Movement from Sweden

2 Which sentence is NOT needed in the passage?

① ⓐ   ② ⓑ   ③ ⓒ   ④ ⓓ

3 What does the underlined sentence mean?

① We can express our opinions on plogging online.

② The internet enables us to start plogging outside.

③ People all around the world are participating in plogging.

④ Plogging is a popular topic both in real life and on the internet.

4 What is the best choice for blank (A)?

① emptying trash cans

② jogging on a clean beach

③ walking to their office in Sweden

④ cleaning up their neighborhoods

5 It's clear why plogging is getting more and more popular because _____.

6 Write T if the statement is true and F if it's false.

(1) The word "plogging" came from an English word and a Swedish phrase.

(2) Erik Ahlström started plogging after noticing other people's actions.

Reading 2

Are you worried about the environment but don't know how to save it? Consider some exciting movements from around the world. Plastic Free July was first started in Australia. During this event, people use and throw away less plastic by reusing daily items like coffee cups and metal straws. By doing this for ⁵ one month, they can build healthy habits and keep their streets, oceans, and communities clean. Disco Soup Day is an event from Germany for reducing food waste. Supermarkets, restaurants, and farms often have a lot of unused food. So on that day, volunteers gather the food and use it to cook delicious meals. These campaigns don't just tell people to reduce waste—they have people celebrate it! ¹⁰ There's nothing better than having fun while saving the earth.

What is the best title for the passage?

① Turning Waste into Daily Items

② Fun Events That Help Our Planet

③ Reusing Does Not Save the Earth

④ Unused Food: A Growing Problem

⑤ Does Plastic Cause Environmental Problems?

10

Summary / Graphic Organizer

A Choose the correct words to fill in the blanks.

movement	trash	jogging	environment	picking up	running

Reading 1

The word "plogging" comes from the English word "_____" and the Swedish phrase *plocka upp*, which means "pick up." It refers to the act of _____ garbage while you are jogging. The idea for plogging came from a Swedish man named Erik Ahlström. He started picking up _____ on the street when he went to work. Before long, he even started doing it on his daily runs. Now, the plogging _____ has spread around the world, and it has become popular on social media.

Reading 2

There are many fun ways for people to help save the _____, such as participating in Plastic Free July in Australia and Disco Soup Day in Germany.

Vocabulary

B Choose the correct word for each definition.

reduce	opinion	empty	event	last	global	environment

1 to become or make smaller in size, price, or amount: _____

2 to keep on existing or happening for a certain amount of time: _____

3 about or involving the whole world: _____

4 the air, water, and land surrounding all living things: _____

5 someone's own thoughts and feelings about something: _____

6 to take out everything inside of something: _____

UNIT 02 Society

• Before Reading   What do you usually do to relieve stress?

Reading 1

For the past week, Mark has been staying up late every night working on a big company presentation. He is so tired that he can barely keep his eyes open. He used to like this job, but lately there is nothing he enjoys about it. He's starting to feel depressed. This is an example of "burnout 5 syndrome." Many people experience this when they work too hard for a very long time. Since the mid-1970s, scientists have been studying about burnout so that they can help workers manage their stress.

Any job can cause stress, but are there certain jobs that 10 really stress people out? Yes! People who work closely with other people, such as teachers, nurses, and police officers, often report feeling burned out. In addition, people with jobs that require them to work irregular hours are also at risk.

That's why _____(A)_____ are important. When employees feel respected, motivated, and trusted, they enjoy their work more. Also, bosses who can identify 15 the signs of burnout will be better able to help those who have it. Burnout is a serious condition, but it can be overcome through good communication and a strong support group.

1   **What is the best title for the passage?**

① The General Symptoms of Depression

② How to Make a Successful Presentation

③ Burnout: Its Causes and How to Overcome It

④ The Importance of Communication in the Workplace

2   **What is mentioned as a reason for "burnout syndrome"?**

① a small office space at work

② working hard for a long period

③ dissatisfaction with a low salary

④ competition between coworkers

3   **Scientists have been researching burnout syndrome in order to**

_____ .

4   **According to the passage, who is LEAST likely to experience burnout syndrome?**

① a waiter who works late at night

② an employee who often works overtime

③ a doctor who examines many different patients

④ a freelance photographer who usually works alone

5   **What is the best choice for blank (A)?**

① training sessions

② professional skills

③ work environments

④ reduced working hours

6   **Write T if the statement is true and F if it's false.**

(1) If a boss knows about the symptoms of burnout, he or she can help those who have it.

(2) Burnout syndrome is very serious, so it is almost impossible to cure it.

Because of the stress of studying, even young students can experience burnout syndrome. However, there are ways to prevent it. First, it's important to do tasks in the order of their importance. (ⓐ) This will help you manage your time well. (ⓑ) During this time, you can relax, exercise, or even meet friends. ₅ (ⓒ) This will reduce your stress levels and help you to be more productive when you start studying again. (ⓓ) At first, you might feel guilty about not studying during this time. (ⓔ) However, without this free time, you could easily burn out.

Do First   Do Next   Do Later

Where would the following sentence best fit?

It's also important to take some time for yourself.

① ⓐ   ② ⓑ   ③ ⓒ   ④ ⓓ   ⑤ ⓔ

Summary / Graphic Organizer

A Choose the correct words to fill in the blanks.

trusted	prevent	communication	irregular	cause	hard

Reading 1

Causes of Burnout Syndrome
- working too _____ for a very long time
- working closely with other people
- jobs that require working _____ hours

▼

How to Overcome It
- make work environments where workers feel respected and _____
- have good _____ and a strong support group

Reading 2

Students can _____ burnout syndrome if they do important tasks first and take some free time for themselves.

Vocabulary

B Complete each sentence with the best word.

order	identify	experience	closely	employee	trust	guilty

1 I heard that her company provides a smartphone to each _____.

2 The students should line up in _____ of shortest to tallest.

3 We are trying to _____ the causes of the problem.

4 Smoking heavily is _____ related to mouth and lung cancer.

5 Elderly people tend to _____ depression when they lose their job.

6 I felt _____ about not spending enough time with my parents.

• **Before Reading** How do you feel when you ride a Ferris wheel at an amusement park?

Reading 1

These days, Ferris wheels are popular rides at amusement parks. They are large, upright wheels, and they have passenger cars around the edge for people to ride in. As the wheel rotates, passengers get a great view of the park. 5

(ⓐ) The very first Ferris wheel was invented in 1893 by George W.G. Ferris. (ⓑ) Ferris was an engineer, and he wanted to build something amazing for the World's Fair in Chicago, Illinois. (ⓒ) He hoped his invention would be as famous as the Eiffel Tower. (ⓓ) 10

The Ferris wheel was especially impressive because of its _____(A)_____. Modern Ferris wheels usually have 20 passenger cars, and each one can only hold a few people. But the original wheel had 36 large passenger cars, and each one had 60 seats. So 2,160 people could ride it at once! The problem, however, was that it was very expensive to operate, so it was only used until 1906. The metal from the wheel 15 was later recycled, and it was used to build the USS Illinois battleship in World War I.

_____(B)_____ the original Ferris wheel is gone, it inspired 20 many people. And now, you can find similar rides at carnivals, fairs, and amusement parks 25 around the world.

1 **What is the passage mainly about?**

① the history of the first Ferris wheel

② interesting inventions from World's Fairs

③ the way the Ferris wheel beat the Eiffel Tower

④ the person who operated the first Ferris wheel

2 **Where would the following sentence best fit?**

And luckily, it was a huge success at the fair.

① ⓐ   ② ⓑ   ③ ⓒ   ④ ⓓ

3 **What is the best choice for blank (A)?**

① size   ② shape

③ weight   ④ material

4 **It can be inferred from the 3rd paragraph that** _____.

① the Ferris wheel could not be used until 1906

② modern Ferris wheels are recycled from the USS Illinois battleship

③ the first Ferris wheel was shut down because of its operating cost

④ modern Ferris wheels are designed to hold more people than the first one

5 **What is the best choice for blank (B)?**

① Unless   ② Once

③ Although   ④ Because

6 **Write T if the statement is true and F if it's false.**

(1) People can get a great view of an amusement park by riding a Ferris wheel.

(2) The Ferris wheel was named after the fair where it was first introduced.

Amusement parks have brought joy to their guests for many years. In fact, the very first amusement park, called Bakken, was founded in Copenhagen, Denmark in 1583!

(A) This attracted circuses and moving rides to the place and made it a proper amusement park. These days, Bakken is still open, and guests can enjoy rides 5 such as the Ferris wheel and an 82-year-old roller coaster!

(B) At that time, a woman discovered a spring in a forest near the city. Copenhagen's water wasn't clean, so many people started visiting the spring for water. Soon after, it became a popular place for entertainers and salesmen who were hoping for more business. 10

(C) The area's fame grew quickly, but it didn't become a proper amusement park until much later. In 1885, buildings and tents were built, and the park was powered by electricity.

Choose the best order of (A), (B), and (C) after the given text.

① (A) – (C) – (B)

② (B) – (A) – (C)

③ (B) – (C) – (A)

④ (C) – (A) – (B)

⑤ (C) – (B) – (A)

Summary / Graphic Organizer

A Choose the correct words to fill in the blanks.

expensive	attracted	invented	spring	famous	similar

Reading 1

In 1893, the first Ferris wheel was _____ by George W.G. Ferris.
– He wanted his invention to be as _____ as the Eiffel Tower.
– The Ferris wheel was really huge, so it could hold 2,160 people at once.

▼

In 1906, the Ferris wheel was not used anymore because of its _____ operating cost.
– Later it was recycled and used to build a battleship for World War I.

▼

Now, Ferris wheels _____ to the first one are found around the world.

Reading 2

Bakken gained popularity as a(n) _____ and later became the first amusement park in the world.

Vocabulary

B Choose the correct word for each definition.

fame	discover	joy	found	weight	rotate	edge

1 great happiness: _____

2 to start something like a business: _____

3 to move around in a circle around a center point: _____

4 the outer or furthest part of something: _____

5 to find something for the first time: _____

6 the state of being well-known and talked about: _____

Sports

How much do you know about what a soccer referee does?

Reading 1

Michael Beal, a professional soccer referee in England's Premier League, tells us about his job.

Q _____ (A) _____

A The main job of a referee is to control the game. You have to make sure the players follow the rules. If they break ⁵ the rules, you have to give a penalty. Sometimes your decisions change the results of the game.

Q What are the good things about your job? Are there any bad things?

A (ⓐ) The best thing is I can watch soccer games closely. ¹⁰ (ⓑ) Of course, there are bad things too, such as stress. (ⓒ) Players, coaches, and fans yell at you and even attack you if they don't agree with your decision. (ⓓ) But I think there are more good things about the job than bad things.

Q _____ (B) _____

A You have to understand the rules of the game. That's why there are many referees ¹⁵ who used to be players. Also, you need to be fit because you run throughout the whole game. And finally, you have to be able to make decisions quickly about unexpected events.

Q _____ (C) _____

A Well, to be a professional referee, you must go to school. A lot of training is ²⁰ necessary. And in soccer, you need more than ten years of experience before you can get a job in a national league.

1 What is the interview mainly about?

① working as a referee

② how to train referees

③ the origin of referees

④ why referees are popular

2 Match the correct question to blanks (A)~(C).

(1) (A) •   • ① What skills does a referee need to have?

(2) (B) •   • ② How does someone become a referee?

(3) (C) •   • ③ What does a referee have to do during a game?

3 Where would the following sentence best fit?

This is fun for me because I really love soccer.

① ⓐ   ② ⓑ   ③ ⓒ   ④ ⓓ

4 Many referees used to be players, and this helps them to

_____.

5 According to the interview, how does Michael feel about his job?

① bored

② relaxed

③ satisfied

④ uninterested

6 What is NOT true about referees?

① They give a penalty if the rules are not followed during the game.

② They sometimes make decisions that are not welcomed by people.

③ They usually make decisions after the game is over.

④ They need at least ten years of experience to work in a national league.

Here are some tools used by soccer referees during a game:

Whistles

Referees use the loud sound of a whistle to control the game. A short whistle is used to show there was a simple foul. A longer, louder whistle means there was a serious foul. Long, loud whistles are also used when ⁵ a goal is scored.

Watches

A watch is used to keep the time of a game. Most referees use two watches. One keeps track of how much time has passed and the other keeps track of time spent for injuries. ¹⁰

Foul Cards

Yellow cards are used to warn players who break the rules. Red cards are used to tell players that they've been thrown out of the game.

Coins

Referees flip a coin at the start of the game. This decides who starts ¹⁵ with the ball and which goal each team will defend.

Flags

Assistant referees carry flags. They raise them in the air to show that the ball went off the field or that there was a foul.

What is NOT true about how referees use their tools?

① Referees blow their whistles after a foul or a goal.

② One of the referee's watches is to check the time spent on injured players.

③ There are two kinds of foul cards, and each has a different meaning.

④ A coin is used to decide which team will kick the ball first at the beginning.

⑤ When the ball goes off the field, flags are lowered by assistant referees.

Summary / Graphic Organizer

A Choose the correct words to fill in the blanks.

disagree	experience	controlling	penalty	rules

Reading 1

Soccer referees have a very important job. They are responsible for _____ the game and making it fair for both teams. If a player breaks the rules, the referee has to give that player a(n) _____. The people involved in the game, such as players, coaches, and even spectators, often _____ with the referee's decisions. In order to be successful, referees need to be familiar with the _____ of soccer. They should also be physically fit because they need to follow the ball up and down the field.

Vocabulary

B Complete each sentence with the best word.

assistant	warn	defend	unexpected	attacked	national	referee

1 If a team cannot _____ their goal well, they will not win.

2 He needed a(n) _____ manager to help him with his work.

3 After a player was tackled, the _____ called a foul.

4 A(n) _____ storm caused them to cancel the tennis match.

5 In May, France has a(n) _____ holiday to celebrate the end of World War II.

6 Many people were _____ by bees in the forest.

Reading 1

Have you ever eaten a delicious meal and then let out a big burp? Your parents probably scolded you and said, "Don't burp! It's rude." But is it possible to stop a burp? And what exactly is a burp, anyway?

Well, a burp is the sound of air escaping from your stomach. To leave your mouth, it must pass a thin muscle at the back of your throat. When air from your stomach rushes past this muscle... uh-oh... BURP! There's really no way to stop it!

So how does air get into your stomach? Well, without knowing it, you usually swallow a liter of air every hour. You swallow even more when you eat and drink. So, burping is perfectly normal. In fact, in some countries, it is polite to burp after eating to show your appreciation to the cook!

_____(A)_____, too much burping can be embarrassing. But don't worry! Here are some ways to burp less often. First, don't talk with your mouth full. Talking and eating at the same time makes you swallow more air. Second, eat slowly. Eating fast pushes more air down into your stomach. Third, stop drinking soda. Since one can of soda has over 18 million air bubbles in it, drinking it may keep you burping for hours!

1   **What is the best title for the passage?**

① Basic Table Manners

② Burping: It's Only Natural!

③ How to Control Loud Burps

④ Exercises for Breathing Correctly

2   **Which of the following mainly causes burps?**

① the air you have swallowed

② the movements of your muscles

③ the time that you eat your meals

④ the gas from what you have eaten

3   **In some countries, burping after a meal is thought of as a polite way of _____.**

4   **What is the best choice for blank (A)?**

① For example

② Therefore

③ However

④ Moreover

5   **According to the passage, who is LEAST likely to burp?**

① "I don't enjoy sweet desserts such as chocolate."

② "I don't think it's rude to talk when my mouth is full."

③ "I'm always in a hurry. I usually finish my lunch within 10 minutes."

④ "Cola is one of my favorite drinks! I drink it almost every day!"

6   **Write T if the statement is true and F if it's false.**

(1) A burping sound is made when air passes through your throat.

(2) There's little chance of swallowing air while you're eating.

It's not only humans that burp. Cows burp often because they eat grass all day. (ⓐ) In fact, just one cow burps out around 150 liters of methane gas per day. (ⓑ) This is a problem because methane gas increases global warming. (ⓒ) It may surprise you to know that a group of cows produces as much methane gas as a family car. (ⓓ) They found that clover and other green leaves cause cows to burp less than grass does. (ⓔ) Luckily, cows love eating those too!

Where would the following sentence best fit?

So scientists are working on a new diet for cows that will reduce their burps.

① ⓐ ② ⓑ ③ ⓒ ④ ⓓ ⑤ ⓔ

Summary / Graphic Organizer

A Choose the correct words to fill in the blanks.

reduces natural increases polite global warming stomach

Reading 1

In many countries, it's not _____ to burp at the dinner table. However, burping is perfectly _____. It happens when air suddenly leaves your _____. This air rushes past a thin muscle in your throat, making an embarrassing sound. About one liter of air enters your stomach every hour. But this amount _____ if you talk while you're eating, eat quickly, or drink soda. By avoiding these things, you'll be able to burp less often.

Reading 2

Burps from cows can increase _____, so scientists are creating a new diet to help cows burp less.

Vocabulary

B Choose the correct word for each definition.

burp embarrassing swallow cause normal rush rude

1 regular; not strange: _____

2 to make something happen: _____

3 to make a loud noise when air comes up through the throat: _____

4 making you feel ashamed, nervous, or uncomfortable: _____

5 not caring or respecting other people or their feelings: _____

6 to make something go into your mouth and to your stomach: _____

• Before Reading   How would you feel if you had to spend a night in prison?

Reading 1

I love to travel, but I'm not a regular tourist. I'm interested in visiting historical sites where terrible things happened. So I went to two sites during my summer vacation.

The first site was Karosta Prison in the European country of Latvia. In the past, it was used as a military ⁵ prison by the Nazis and Russians. But today it's a hotel. Even though I was a guest, I was treated like a prisoner! The hotel employees dressed like prison guards and punished me when I did not listen to them. It was a lot of fun but also a little ____(A)____ . I was very ____(B)____ when I ¹⁰ checked out and was free again!

I also visited the Robben Island Prison Museum in South Africa. Political prisoners used to be kept there. (ⓐ) I took a tour of the island and the prison. (ⓑ) My tour guide was a former prisoner! (ⓒ) He also showed me the small cell that Nelson Mandela lived in for eighteen years. (ⓓ) It was an amazing trip! ¹⁵

You might think it is strange to visit these places. But I think it is an educational experience. We need to learn about dark events in human history so we can stop them from happening again.

1   What is the passage mainly about?

① protecting historical sites

② tourist attractions in South Africa

③ interesting hotels around the world

④ traveling to places where bad things happened

2   What is the best pair for blanks (A) and (B)?

① exciting   —   calm

② noisy   —   curious

③ scary   —   relieved

④ depressing —   shocked

3   What can be inferred from the 2nd paragraph?

① The hotel employees are former prisoners.

② Latvia may have once been ruled by Russia.

③ Foreign visitors must pay more to stay at the hotel.

④ People can stay in the hotel only as part of a group.

4   Where would the following sentence best fit?

He told me about his personal experiences.

① ⓐ   ② ⓑ   ③ ⓒ   ④ ⓓ

5   Why does the writer mention that <u>it is strange to visit these places</u>?

① because they are extremely expensive

② because they are unusual places for a vacation

③ because the people there speak different languages

④ because they are far away from where the writer lives

6   The writer thinks people need to learn about dark events in order to _____.

9/11 Ground Zero Tour

9/11 Memorial

We invite you to visit the 9/11 Memorial. It was built on Ground Zero, the area where the Twin Towers used to stand. Here, you can read the names of those who lost their lives in the 9/11 attacks, which happened on September 11th, 2001.

Tour Highlights

- 90-minute English-language tour of Ground Zero and the 9/11 Memorial
- Led by New Yorkers who were directly affected by 9/11
- Learn more about the events of that day and the heroes of 9/11

Tour Policy

- Please arrive ten minutes early. If you are late, you may not be able to join the group.
- Tell the guide your name. Printed tickets are not needed.

Rescheduling Policy

- You can reschedule your tour at any time with no penalty.
- No refund is available if you decide not to take the tour after rescheduling it.

What is NOT true about the 9/11 Ground Zero Tour?

① It includes a visit to the place where the Twin Towers were.

② It takes an hour and half for the tour of Ground Zero and the memorial.

③ You should arrive on time, as your group may leave without you.

④ You need to bring a printed ticket with your name on it.

⑤ You cannot get a refund after changing your tour schedule.

Summary / Graphic Organizer

A Choose the correct words to fill in the blanks.

hotel	political	history	punish	educational	prisoners

Reading 1

I like to visit places where tragic events took place. In Latvia, tourists can stay in a(n) _____ that used to be a prison. The staff treats the guests like _____, and they even _____ the guests when they don't listen. In South Africa, tourists can visit Robben Island Prison Museum. Some of the tour guides are former _____ prisoners. People who visit this museum can see Nelson Mandela's prison cell. Even though visiting these sorts of places can be strange and scary, it's very _____.

Vocabulary

B Complete each sentence with the best word.

educational	site	policy	directly	rescheduled	refund	personal

1 Some doctors say that sleeping well is _____ related to your health.

2 The teacher showed his students a(n) _____ movie during class.

3 Please bring your purchase back within 10 days if you want a full _____.

4 Due to bad weather, the trip to Paris was _____ for next week.

5 The _____ for entering the theater has changed.

6 The author wrote a book based on his _____ experiences.

• Before Reading What do you do to stop yourself from feeling nervous?

Reading 1

Dear Dr. Kay,

Every time I meet someone new, I feel very small and can't think of anything to say. I also get very nervous if the teacher asks me a question during class. My cheeks turn bright red. How can I stop being so shy?   5

Shy Guy

First of all, remember that _____(A)_____.
Many people need some time to become comfortable with new people and situations. But if you really want to overcome your shyness, try these useful tips.   10

First, _____(B)_____. Ask simple questions like, "What did you do today?" They will love to answer your questions, and the conversation will continue easily. Second, practice what you want to say. ⓐYou can even write down some ideas and practice them in your room. ⓑMemorize some things like "It's lovely to meet you" or "The weather's great today, isn't it?" ⓒMost people have at least one   15 thing that they enjoy doing in their free time. ⓓThen when you meet someone new, you'll be able to easily talk to them. Third, give yourself a chance! Many shy people get angry with themselves. This only makes them more nervous. Instead of blaming yourself, take a deep breath and encourage yourself. You will feel better immediately! Finally, remember that you are a unique and special person. Your shyness is just one   20 part of you! Find your own style, because others will like you for just being you.

Dr. Kay

1 **What is Dr. Kay's advice mainly about?**

① how to deal with shyness

② tips for making new friends

③ ways to overcome your anger

④ the importance of listening to others

2 **What is the best choice for blank (A)?**

① everyone likes to be alone

② shy people are not popular

③ being shy isn't a bad thing

④ your shyness can annoy others

3 **What is the best choice for blank (B)?**

① count how many friends you have

② practice saying things very loudly

③ understand other people's situations

④ start small conversations with people you know

4 **Which sentence is NOT needed in the passage?**

① ⓐ   ② ⓑ   ③ ⓒ   ④ ⓓ

5 **What is Shy Guy UNLIKELY to do to overcome his shyness if he follows the advice?**

① practice talking with close friends often

② bring small presents to give to others

③ write down some friendly greetings

④ try to calm down when he gets mad at himself

6 **What is the meaning of the underlined part?**

① Shyness is not good.

② Be a creative speaker.

③ A friend can change your life.

④ Love yourself the way you are.

As you step onto the school bus, you trip and fall. Everyone starts to laugh, and your face turns as red as a tomato! Don't worry. We all blush sometimes. But what exactly is blushing?

When you feel embarrassed, your brain makes a special 5 chemical. This chemical widens the blood vessels in your face. More blood flows through them, and your skin turns bright red! Studies show that blushing is most common among teenagers, who feel embarrassed more often than adults do.

So, is it possible to control blushing? Not really. But by being 10 more confident, you can reduce the feelings of embarrassment that cause it.

To summarize the passage, what is the best choice for blanks (A) and (B)?

> When people are _____ (A) _____ they blush because more blood flows through
> the blood vessels in their face, and this can't be _____ (B) _____ .

	(A)		(B)
①	laughing	—	possible
②	confident	—	reduced
③	embarrassed	—	controlled
④	confident	—	controlled
⑤	embarrassed	—	possible

34

Summary / Graphic Organizer

A Choose the correct words to fill in the blanks.

| angry | start | listen to | be | shy | write down |

Reading 1

| Problem | I feel very _____ when I meet someone new or say something in front of people. |

▼

Solutions	1. _____ small talk with people you know.
	2. _____ things you want to say.
	3. Try not to get _____ at yourself.
	4. Just _____ yourself.

Vocabulary

B Choose the correct word for each definition.

| memorize | overcome | encourage | unique | widen | confident | blush |

1 feeling sure in your own or other's abilities: _____

2 to try to help someone feel that they can do something: _____

3 to successfully deal with a problem or a feeling: _____

4 very special, unusual, or good: _____

5 to learn something to remember it: _____

6 to become red in the face due to embarrassment or shyness: _____

UNIT 08 Literature

Reading 1

Anne is a young Jewish girl. When Nazi Germans take over her country, she is forced into hiding. So she begins writing in her diary...

TUESDAY, NOVEMBER 10, 1942

Dear Kitty,

_____(A)_____ news! An eighth person is joining us in hiding! We've always thought there was room and food for another person. However, we were worried about giving too much work to the people who help us hide. Recently, there's been some news about more and more horrible things happening to Jews, though. So Father decided to ask our protectors about hiding one more person. Thankfully, they agreed and said, "There's little difference between seven and eight people." So we all sat down to think about who we could add to our growing family. This wasn't difficult. Father rejected all his friend's relatives, so we chose his other friend's dentist instead. Currently, the dentist lives with a young Christian lady. ⓐ While we don't know him well, he seems to be a quiet but kind gentleman. ⓑ All gentlemen should behave politely. ⓒ We're sure he'll fit in. ⓓ If he comes, he'll sleep in my room, so my sister will have to use the folding bed. Because one of my teeth has been hurting, we'll ask him to bring his dentist tools too!

Yours, Anne

1 What is the best choice for blank (A)?

① Funny

② Great

③ Terrible

④ Annoying

2 Why did Anne's father suggest taking another person into their hiding group?

① Anne's sister bought a new folding bed.

② He wanted someone to help their protectors.

③ Anne needed a dentist to take care of her teeth.

④ So many horrible things had happened to Jews lately.

3 What does the underlined sentence mean?

① There are enough people to help a new person.

② Hiding one more person would not be a problem.

③ The protectors can accept up to seven more people.

④ Anne's father would have to pay more to their protectors.

4 Which sentence is NOT needed in the passage?

① ⓐ   ② ⓑ   ③ ⓒ   ④ ⓓ

5 What is NOT suggested in the passage?

① Currently, there are seven people hiding together.

② The people hiding together discussed who would hide with them.

③ Anne's father didn't want to hide his friend's relatives.

④ Anne's father used to be the dentist's patient.

6 Write T if the statement is true and F if it's false.

(1) The people in hiding didn't want to give too much work to their protectors.

(2) The dentist is living alone now.

The Diary of Anne Frank is the journal of a teenage Jewish girl. It tells about her family's time in hiding during World War II. Before the war, Anne's family had moved to the Netherlands to escape Nazi Germans. But Germany attacked the Netherlands in 1940, so Anne's family was in danger once again. ⓐ To hide, her family found a secret place in Amsterdam and started living there on July 5 6, 1942. ⓑ Anne often wrote in her diary during this time and described her family's experiences. ⓒ She was known for being confident and talkative, unlike her sister who was very quiet. ⓓ The last time she wrote was on August 1, 1944, and the Nazi German police found their hiding place three days later. ⓔ In 1947, two years after her death, Anne's diary was published so that the world would 10 know her story.

Which sentence is NOT needed in the passage?

① ⓐ   ② ⓑ   ③ ⓒ   ④ ⓓ   ⑤ ⓔ

Summary / Graphic Organizer

A Choose the correct words to fill in the blanks.

| dentist | join | horrible | father | hiding | reject | share |

Reading 1

Anne was a young Jewish girl. She was hiding from Nazi Germans with six other Jewish people. At that time, _____ things were being done to Jewish people. So Anne's _____ asked their protectors to hide one more person. Their protectors agreed, so the people hiding together discussed who would _____ them. They finally decided to invite a _____. He would _____ a room with Anne, and they would ask him to bring his dentist tools to check Anne's teeth.

Reading 2

The Diary of Anne Frank is about a Jewish girl's experience _____ from Nazi Germans during World War II.

Vocabulary

B Complete each sentence with the best word.

| journal | horrible | reject | force | talkative | hide | relative |

1 He kept a _____ while he was traveling in Australia.

2 She is usually quiet but becomes _____ on the phone.

3 You can't _____ me to stay in my room.

4 The coffee smelled nice but tasted _____.

5 James is my close _____.

6 I felt so embarrassed that I wanted to _____ in a hole.

Reading 1

People often love or hate technological advancements. Well, how about self-service kiosks in grocery stores and restaurants? People use kiosks to select or scan items and then buy them by themselves. But what do they think about them? 5

Some people support the use of self-service kiosks. First of all, kiosks let people wait less and check out faster, so more people can quickly finish their shopping. Secondly, kiosks improve the accuracy of orders because people can choose exactly what they want. Even employers benefit, as 10 they can spend less money on paying employees. Few employees are needed to help customers with the kiosks.

On the other hand, others oppose the use of these kiosks. For one, customers can feel frustrated when kiosks are hard to use or even stop working. (ⓐ) Then workers have to come and fix the problem. (ⓑ) In addition, cashiers are skilled 15 workers who can efficiently check out items. (ⓒ) Furthermore, kiosks make customers do all the work of scanning and bagging. (ⓓ) Maybe you should 20 get paid to shop!

Technology is always changing and growing. But, that isn't always a good thing. It's important to consider the users' various needs before we change 25 how we live.

1 **What is the best title for the passage?**

① How to Communicate with Customers

② How We Shop Changes How We Live!

③ Do You Like or Dislike Self-Service Kiosks?

④ Why Some People Refuse to Use New Technologies

2 **What is mentioned as a benefit of using self-service kiosks? (Choose two.)**

① People spend less money on shopping.

② People save time because they don't have to wait as long.

③ Orders become more accurate.

④ People are happy to scan and bag items themselves.

3 **When might the customers feel frustrated using self-service kiosks?**

_____

4 **Where would the following sentence best fit?**

> So the lines for the cashiers move fast.

① ⓐ   ② ⓑ   ③ ⓒ   ④ ⓓ

5 **What does the underlined sentence mean?**

① Customers can have their own shops.

② The employer will hire customers as cashiers.

③ Customers are doing what employees did before.

④ Customers should pay money to use self-service kiosks.

6 **Write T if the statement is true and F it's false.**

(1) People can scan items and pay by themselves at the grocery store using kiosks.

(2) It's important to consider the cashier's skill when we decide to use new technology.

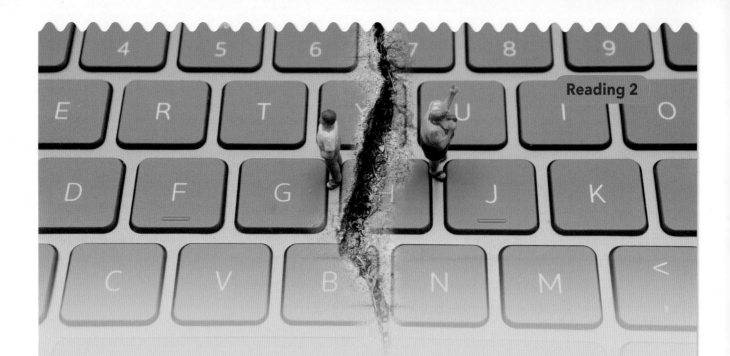

Some people have _____ and the ability to use them, while others do not. This gap is called the digital divide. The term includes both the financial and technical ability to use technology. This divide exists between developed and underdeveloped countries as well as between the educated and the uneducated. Generally, more chances are available to those 5 who are used to technology. On the other hand, people with limited access have fewer ways of communicating with others and fewer job options. Also, with the increase in online education, those who lack internet resources are often unable to develop their skills. Obviously, technology has become a more important part of the world. So, improved government policies and educational programs will 10 be necessary to solve this issue.

What is the best choice for the blank?

① the skills to understand digital data

② ideas about solving problems online

③ easy access to internet services and technology

④ the resources to get a job related to internet services

⑤ knowledge and information on educational programs

Summary / Graphic Organizer

A Choose the correct words to fill in the blanks.

| check out | accurate | reduce | frustrated | fast | skilled |

Reading 1

The Use of Self-Service Kiosks

For
1. People wait less and _____ faster.
2. The order is more _____.
3. Employers spend less money on employees.

Against
1. Customers feel _____ when they fail to use kiosks easily.
2. Waiting in line for cashiers is _____.
3. Customers should scan and bag their items by themselves.

Reading 2

Government policies and educational programs are needed to _____ the digital divide, the gap between those with easy internet access and those without it.

Vocabulary

B Choose the correct word for each definition.

| exist | support | hate | knowledge | term | select | refuse |

1 to appear somewhere: _____

2 to say you won't do or accept something: _____

3 to choose from a group: _____

4 to help or encourage a person or thing: _____

5 a word or phrase used to describe something: _____

6 information and skills from education or experience: _____

• Before Reading　Do you know what nonprofit organizations do?

Reading 1

I'm an eye doctor, but I don't work in an office or a normal hospital like most eye doctors. In fact, the hospital where I work is the only one of its kind in the world. It's the "Flying Eye Hospital," a hospital on an airplane! Since 1982 this airplane hospital has been run by ORBIS, a nonprofit ⁵ organization.

_____(A)_____ Many poor countries don't have the right equipment or facilities to give the best eye care. In some areas, there aren't any hospitals at all! So we have to bring all the equipment we ¹⁰ need with us wherever we go.

We have treated millions of people in many countries, such as Bangladesh, Ethiopia, and India. Being able to help so many people really makes our work worthwhile. Like me, all the other people who work for ORBIS are volunteers. This includes everyone from the nurses to the pilots. ¹⁵

_____(B)_____ giving free medical care, ORBIS doctors give training to local doctors in the flying hospital. This is important. It means that even after we leave a country, people can still get eye care from their local doctors.

1   **What is the best title for the passage?**

① Fun Medical Care for Kids

② Overcoming Eye Diseases

③ The Joy of Volunteer Work

④ The Eye Hospital That Can Fly

2   **What is the best choice for blank (A)?**

① Where has the ORBIS eye hospital visited?

② Who suggested the idea of a flying hospital?

③ Why does the ORBIS eye hospital need to be on a plane?

④ How many people are working for the ORBIS eye hospital?

3   **What is the best choice for blank (B)?**

① Because of   ② Instead of

③ Thanks to   ④ In addition to

4   **What can be inferred from the 4th paragraph?**

① ORBIS believes doctors are needed to fly the airplane.

② The medical training program is very popular with local doctors.

③ Local doctors are interested in working in the ORBIS eye hospital.

④ The work ORBIS does has both short-term and long-term benefits.

5   **How does the writer feel about his job at ORBIS?**

① It's dangerous.

② It's meaningful.

③ It's challenging.

④ It's uninteresting.

6   **What is NOT true about the ORBIS eye hospital?**

① It is run by a nonprofit organization.

② All of its members are volunteers.

③ It collects money to build local hospitals.

④ It gives free care to people in poor countries.

You've probably heard of the Red Cross. What about Greenpeace, Amnesty International, and Doctors Without Borders?

(A) When there's a disaster anywhere in the world, for example, the Red Cross and Doctors Without Borders can go there and save lives.

(B) In a similar way, Greenpeace works to help the environment, and Amnesty ₅ International protects human rights. There are also millions of smaller NGOs all around the world. Almost all of these need volunteers. So why not volunteer with one?

(C) They are all well-known NGOs. NGO stands for non-governmental organization. These organizations help people in ways governments are ₁₀ unable to.

Choose the best order of (A), (B), and (C) after the given text.

① (A) – (C) – (B)

② (B) – (A) – (C)

③ (B) – (C) – (A)

④ (C) – (A) – (B)

⑤ (C) – (B) – (A)

Summary / Graphic Organizer

A   Choose the correct words to fill in the blanks.

plane   trains   government   volunteers   thanks   treated

Reading 1

ORBIS is a nonprofit organization that runs a hospital located on a _____. Known as the "Flying Eye Hospital," it travels to poor countries all around the world where people can't get eye care. And this amazing hospital has already _____ millions of people. Furthermore, all of the people who work for ORBIS are _____, including the pilots. ORBIS also _____ local doctors in the countries it visits so that patients can still get good care after the Flying Eye Hospital leaves.

Reading 2

Non-government organizations help people and the environment in ways that the _____ can't, but they need volunteers to help them.

Vocabulary

B   Complete each sentence with the best word.

border   medical   normal   nonprofit   similar   volunteer   facilities

1 She has taught poor students for many years as a _____.

2 She crossed the _____ from France into Spain.

3 He was badly injured, so he needed _____ care at the hospital.

4 People like this health club because all the _____ here are new and clean.

5 It's _____ to feel tired after walking for so long.

6 The two pictures look very _____, but they're not the same.

Reading 1

Go into any food store in your neighborhood, and you will see lots of colorful bags of potato chips. Available in various flavors, shapes, and sizes, potato chips are a popular choice for snack lovers.

They were invented in 1853 by a cook called George ⁵ Crum at a restaurant near New York. At that time, thick-cut french fries were popular in the US. One day, however, a troublesome customer kept complaining that his french fries were too thick. So Crum decided to teach him a lesson. He sliced some potatoes so thin that they couldn't be eaten ¹⁰ with a fork and gave them to the customer. To Crum's _____(A)_____, the customer loved them! Other customers wanted to try the new snack, and Crum added them to the menu.

(ⓐ) Potato chips soon became popular all around the northeastern US. (ⓑ) They had to be peeled and sliced by hand and stored in wooden barrels. ¹⁵ (ⓒ) However, machines were soon invented that could mass-produce potato chips, and wax-coated bags were developed that could keep them fresh for a long time. (ⓓ)

Perhaps the next time you buy a bag of potato ²⁰ chips from a store, you'll remember the story of how they became such a popular snack.

1 **What is the passage mainly about?**

① why people enjoy potato chips in restaurants

② how technologies for producing snacks developed

③ how American snacks are different from French ones

④ how potato chips were invented and became popular

2 **What does the underlined sentence mean?**

① He decided to stop serving his customers.

② He wanted to get some cooking advice from the man.

③ He decided to teach the man how to cook french fries.

④ He wanted to show the man that he shouldn't complain.

3 **What is the best choice for blank (A)?**

① regret   ② anger

③ surprise   ④ disappointment

4 **It can be inferred from the 2nd paragraph that** _____.

① potato chips were not popular at first

② potato chips were created by chance

③ potato chips taste better with other snacks

④ potato chips are less healthy than french fries

5 **Where would the following sentence best fit?**

But they were not easy to make or store.

① ⓐ   ② ⓑ   ③ ⓒ   ④ ⓓ

6 **Write T if the statement is true and F if it's false.**

(1) It took a long time for Crum to invent his new menu item, potato chips.

(2) At first, potato chips were popular only in some parts of the US.

For hundreds of years, potatoes were the most common food in Britain and North America. Thus it's not surprising that _____. For example, the "meat and potatoes" of something means the most important part of it. On the other hand, "small potatoes" means something unimportant. A "hot potato" is a troublesome topic that nobody wants to talk about. And have ⁵ you heard of a "couch potato"? It is a person who likes to sit and watch TV all day. Then, can you guess what a "mouse potato" is? That's right! It is a person who likes to use the computer all day long!

What is the best choice for the blank?

① many English idioms contain the word "potato"

② the origin of the word "potato" goes back to Europe

③ there are a lot of traditional recipes for potato dishes

④ potatoes are still used in various ways in North America

⑤ English speakers often make jokes using the word "potato"

Summary / Graphic Organizer

A Choose the correct words to fill in the blanks.

| thick | fresh | idioms | loved | peeled | invented | thin |

Reading 1

Potato chips are a popular snack. A man named George Crum _____ them in 1853. He was a cook who often made french fries at his restaurant. One day, a customer complained that his french fries were too _____. Annoyed, Crum sliced some potatoes as _____ as he could and gave them to his customer. Surprisingly, the customer _____ them. Soon, they became very popular. Machines were invented to mass-produce potato chips, which were kept in wax-coated bags to keep them _____.

Reading 2

Because potatoes were the most common food in Britain and North America for many years, a lot of English _____ include the word "potato."

Vocabulary

B Choose the correct word for each definition.

| peel | complain | flavor | idiom | troublesome | slice | store |

1 to say that you are not happy about something: _____

2 the particular taste that a food or drink has: _____

3 to take off the outer covering of something: _____

4 to cut something into thin pieces: _____

5 causing problems or annoyance to someone: _____

6 to keep something somewhere: _____

• Before Reading   Have you ever seen spiders making webs?

Reading 1

Spider webs are everywhere—under your bed, in your closet, and on the ceiling. ⓐ You might not think they're special at all. ⓑ There are only a few spiders that can make humans sick. ⓒ But scientists are very interested in learning more about spider silk, the material they use to make their ⁵ webs. ⓓ It interests people because it's very strong. You can bend or stretch it, but it's hard to break. In some ways, spider silk is stronger than <u>steel</u>!

Scientists are studying how to use the silk to make products. They think it could be used to help police officers ¹⁰ or soldiers. Clothes made from spider silk would protect them from bullets. It could also be used to create better airbags in cars. An airbag made from spider silk would be softer and less harmful to passengers. And lastly, doctors hope to use spider silk to treat deep cuts. The silk could help these cuts stay closed, so they heal faster.

But there's one problem. It's difficult to collect silk from spiders. They like to ¹⁵ spend time alone, so it's impossible to create a "spider farm." Instead, scientists are trying to discover the secret to making spider silk. If they can learn to produce it, it will be possible to create many more useful products.

1   **What is the main point of the passage?**

① The silk from some spiders is hard to get.

② We should study spiders to understand their behavior better.

③ Products made from spider silk will save the lives of many people.

④ Spider silk might be very useful if we could find out how to produce it.

2   **Which sentence is NOT needed in the passage?**

① ⓐ   ② ⓑ   ③ ⓒ   ④ ⓓ

3   **What makes scientists have an interest in spiders?**

① the food they eat

② the shape of their webs

③ the strength of their silk

④ the places they build webs

4   **Why does the writer mention <u>steel</u>?**

① to show how hard a spider's body is

② to emphasize how strong spider silk is

③ to explain how special spider silk can be

④ to introduce the different kinds of spiders

5   **According to the passage, what is NOT something spider silk can be used for?**

① stopping bullets from harming people

② protecting passengers in car accidents

③ helping patients' injuries get better faster

④ keeping people from getting wet in the rain

6   **Spiders can't be kept together in large numbers because they**

_____ .

Many people dislike spiders. They think that all spiders are dangerous, so they kill them without a second thought.

(A) This is because spiders eat insects, including ones that can be harmful to people. Also, it's possible that spider venom—the poison they use to kill insects—could someday be used by farmers to protect their crops. 5

(B) But actually, there are only a few kinds of spiders that can hurt people. Most spiders actually help us.

(C) This would be really helpful because spider venom is natural, so it's safer for humans than dangerous *pesticides. So, don't believe everything you hear about spiders. Next time you see one, don't bother it. Just leave it alone. 10

*pesticide: a chemical used to kill harmful insects

Choose the best order of (A), (B), and (C) after the given text.

① (A) – (C) – (B)

② (B) – (A) – (C)

③ (B) – (C) – (A)

④ (C) – (A) – (B)

⑤ (C) – (B) – (A)

Summary / Graphic Organizer

A Choose the correct words to fill in the blanks.

heal	protect	airbags	stretch	crops	collect

Reading 1	Spider Silk
Characteristic	strength
Possible Uses	– to make clothes to _____ soldiers and police officers from bullets – to make _____ for cars – to help deep cuts _____ faster
Problem and Solution	It is hard to _____ spider silk, so scientists are trying to learn how to make it.

Reading 2

Even though many people dislike spiders, they are helpful to us, and their venom might be useful for protecting _____ in the future.

Vocabulary

B Complete each sentence with the best word.

products	collect	hurt	dislike	bending	stretch	ceiling

1 To make a pizza, you must _____ the dough.

2 You can buy many _____ at this market, from food to kitchen items.

3 I _____ my leg, so I have to go to a hospital.

4 He is so tall that his head almost touches the _____ when he stands.

5 When I saw her, she was _____ down to pick up the paper on the floor.

6 He likes to _____ coins from different countries.

Reading 1

It is March 17th, and you are standing in the middle of a noisy parade. People dance by and clovers are everywhere you look. Then suddenly, someone pinches you! Why would they do that? Well, look around you. Everyone and everything is green. Wow, even the river is flowing with ⁵ green water, and the girl who pinched you is drinking green juice! No, this is not a dream. This is Saint Patrick's Day, and you were pinched for not wearing green.

Saint Patrick's Day is not only about songs, parades, green drinks, and green food. It is a day to celebrate a holy ¹⁰ man who lived in Britain in the 4th century. Taken as a slave to Ireland when he was just 16, Saint Patrick escaped, yet returned years later as a priest. He spent the rest of his life spreading Christianity. But why all the green, you ask? Well, legend has it that he used the three-leaf clover to teach about Christianity.

ⓐ So hurry up and put on something green. ⓑ Then someone around you may ¹⁵ give you a kiss. Why? ⓒ The four-leaf clover is a symbol of good luck. ⓓ On Saint Patrick's Day, it's lucky to kiss a person wearing green!

1 **What is the passage mainly about?**

① a popular musical

② a holiday about luck

③ a costume competition

④ an environmental campaign

2 **What is NOT mentioned about Saint Patrick's Day?**

① when it is

② what people do

③ why it is popular

④ who it celebrates

3 Green is the color of Saint Patrick's Day because ＿＿＿＿＿＿

＿＿＿＿＿＿＿＿＿＿＿＿＿＿＿＿＿＿＿＿＿＿＿.

4 **Which sentence is NOT needed in the passage?**

① ⓐ   ② ⓑ   ③ ⓒ   ④ ⓓ

5 **According to the passage, what is NOT true about Saint Patrick's Day?**

① You can get pinched for not wearing green.

② It is an event in memory of a British priest.

③ You give clovers to everyone you meet.

④ Kissing a person who wears green can give you luck.

6 **How can we describe the mood of the passage?**

① lively

② boring

③ touching

④ mysterious

Come to a Fun Green Party!

The O'Reilly family invites you to a Saint Patrick's Day party!

It starts at 7:00 p.m. next Saturday, March 14th.

You can enjoy traditional Irish food, music, and dancing.

There will be yummy green soda, green cookies, and green candy!

The party will go on for four hours in the backyard. 5

You may bring friends or family members.

There will be a surprise for some lucky guests:

Anyone who finds a four-leaf clover drawn on the bottom of his or her cup

will be given a nice gift!

You don't have to bring anything. 10

Just make sure you wear green!

See you at the party!

What is NOT true about the Green Party?

① There will be traditional Irish food and green-colored snacks.

② It begins at 7:00 p.m. and ends at around 9:00 p.m.

③ It will be hosted in the O'Reilly family's backyard.

④ Whoever has a cup with a four-leaf clover on it gets a surprise gift.

⑤ Guests need to wear something green.

Summary / Graphic Organizer

A Choose the correct words to fill in the blanks.

spreading	pinch	slave	escape	holy

Reading 1

Saint Patrick's Day

What people do on Saint Patrick's Day
- wear green and eat green food
- _____ other people who are not wearing green
- dance, sing, and have parades to celebrate a(n) _____ man

Who Saint Patrick was
- He was a British priest in the 4th century.
- At 16, he was a(n) _____ in Ireland but later became a priest.
- He devoted his life to _____ Christianity.

Vocabulary

B Choose the correct word for each definition.

spread	bottom	noisy	holy	celebrate	surprise	escape

1 to make known to many people: _____

2 to get away from a bad place or situation: _____

3 the lowest or deepest part of something: _____

4 an unexpected thing or event: _____

5 related to a god or religion: _____

6 making much noise: _____

Reading 1

Quick response codes, typically called QR codes, are becoming a popular way to store and share information. ⓐThey are similar to barcodes. ⓑThese days, most QR Codes are scanned with a smartphone. ⓒBut instead of using lines, they use squares and black dots. ⓓYou can find them in many places, including on products and in advertisements. But how do they work?

First, a QR reader identifies a QR code by the three large squares in the corners of the code. Then the reader breaks the code down into smaller sections and examines them. In order to recognize the pattern in each section, the reader measures the amount of light it reflects. This is possible because the color black absorbs light, but white reflects it. Once the patterns are recognized, the information stored in the code can be accessed.

QR codes are incredibly useful. They are convenient to use and provide easy access to large amounts of information. _____(A)_____, they are a great space-saving solution. For example, companies can use QR codes to provide customers with product details and instruction manuals. This way, they don't have to print them on the product's package. With so many uses, it's easy to see why QR codes are now used in almost every industry.

1   **What is the best title for the passage?**

① Barcodes: The Rival of QR Codes

② A New Way to Access Product Details

③ Problems and Solutions in Using QR Codes

④ QR Codes: An Effective Way to Store Information

2   **Which sentence is NOT needed in the passage?**

① ⓐ   ② ⓑ   ③ ⓒ   ④ ⓓ

3   **The QR reader can recognize a QR code because of**

_____.

4   **What is true according to the passage?**

① QR codes are composed of black lines and dots.

② QR readers can measure how much reflected light there is.

③ QR codes require a wide space to function.

④ Using QR codes requires companies to print product details on packages.

5   **What is the best choice for blank (A)?**

① Instead

② In contrast

③ Furthermore

④ Nevertheless

6   **Which of the following is NOT mentioned about QR codes?**

① how they are different from barcodes

② when they were invented

③ how they are recognized

④ what they are used for

In 1994, a Japanese car part company called Denso Wave invented the first QR code. They wanted a better way to keep track of their parts during production. Barcodes had become too limiting for this purpose. They can't hold very much information because they can only be scanned from top to bottom. But QR codes can be scanned from top to bottom and from right to left. This 5 means they can _____. In fact, they can hold up to four thousand characters of text. Since Denso Wave created the QR system, they own the rights to it. However, the company decided not to use these rights. This means anyone can use QR codes freely.

What is the best choice for the blank?

① be created in any shape or size

② easily replace the image with text

③ work with many different scanners

④ access information stored in barcodes

⑤ store a much larger amount of information

A Choose the correct words to fill in the blanks.

| convenient | reflected | information | store | products | patterns |

Reading 1

A QR code, or quick response code, stores and shares _____ in its squares and black dots. A QR reader carefully examines each section of the code by measuring how much light is being _____. This allows the reader to recognize the _____ in the code and access the stored information. Nowadays, QR codes are extremely popular, as they can store plenty of data in this _____ way.

Reading 2

Denso Wave invented the QR code as a way to _____ more information, and the company allows anyone to use this technology freely.

Vocabulary

B Complete each sentence with the best word.

| solution | purpose | rivals | absorb | share | advertisement | identify |

1 The _____ of this campaign is to raise money for the library.

2 We haven't found a good _____ for the problem yet.

3 The two teams are _____ because they play each other often.

4 Let's _____ the big cake with your friends.

5 The _____ helped the company sell a lot of products.

6 They were able to _____ the criminal.

• Before Reading Do you like to listen to music played with string instruments?

Reading 1

Would you believe me if I told you there's a musical instrument worth millions of dollars? It's true. The instrument is a violin called "the Cannon." It was made in 1743 by one of the most famous violinmakers, Giuseppe Guarneri. 5

The Cannon was given its name by Niccolò Paganini, a very talented Italian violinist. He called it this because its sound was so powerful. After receiving the instrument as a gift in 1802, he didn't enjoy playing any other violin. Paganini loved the Cannon more than anything. 10

When Paganini died in 1840, the violin was given to the city of Genoa so it could be taken care of. ⓐEver since then, the Cannon has been kept in Genoa's city hall, where a team of experts has cared for it. ⓑThey repair it when necessary and make sure it is always in top condition. ⓒYou must know a lot about instruments to be an expert. ⓓBecause of this, the violin looks almost the same today as it did in Paganini's time. 15

_____(A)_____, the Cannon is not always kept in a showcase. There is a special event for which it is taken out of city hall. Every two years, a music contest called Premio Paganini is held in Genoa. As a reward, the winner gets to play Paganini's famous violin for one day, which is a great honor. 20

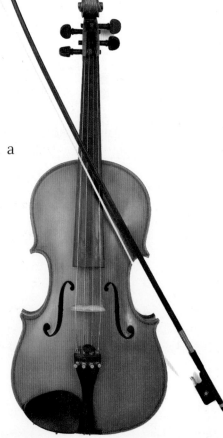

1 What is the passage mainly about?

① how Premio Paganini started

② a famous violin owned by Paganini

③ the great music of Niccolò Paganini

④ the expensive instruments of popular musicians

2 According to the passage, why was the violin called "the Cannon"?

① because of the way it looks

② because of its strong sound

③ because of its maker's name

④ because of the city where it was made

3 Which sentence is NOT needed in the passage?

① ⓐ   ② ⓑ   ③ ⓒ   ④ ⓓ

4 What is the best choice for blank (A)?

① So

② As a result

③ In addition

④ However

5 The winner of Premio Paganini has a chance to _____

_____ .

6 What is NOT true about the Cannon?

① It was made by a well-known violinmaker.

② It was Paganini's second-most favorite violin.

③ It was given to Genoa to be taken care of.

④ It is played on a special day every two years.

Niccolò Paganini was born in Genoa, Italy, in 1782. He gave his first violin concert at the age of 11 and quickly became known as a great musician. Because his playing was so amazing, some people thought Paganini must have sold his soul to the devil. But ⁵ according to researchers, Paganini was a natural-born artist. He had very long fingers, which allowed him to play difficult songs easily. Paganini was a great composer as well. He wrote much of his music for his own performances. Some of his works are still among the most difficult ever written for the violin. ¹⁰

What is the best title for the passage?

① A Mysterious Concert for the Devil

② Paganini: A Musician of Great Talent

③ The Science Behind Playing the Violin

④ What Makes Paganini's Music Hard to Play?

⑤ Becoming a Successful Artist: Talent vs. Effort

Summary / Graphic Organizer

A Choose the correct words to fill in the blanks.

long	kept	winner	powerful	nicknamed	favorite	talented

Reading 1

In 1743, a violinmaker named Giuseppe Guarneri made a violin with a very _____ sound. It was given to the violinist Niccolò Paganini, who _____ it "the Cannon." The Cannon was Paganini's _____ instrument, and when he died in 1840, it was given to the city of Genoa. Today, the violin is worth millions of dollars and is _____ in a showcase in Genoa's city hall. Every two years, the lucky _____ of a music contest is allowed to play the Cannon for one day.

Reading 2

Niccolò Paganini was an amazing violin player and composer, and he could easily play difficult songs because of his natural talent and his _____ fingers.

Vocabulary

B Choose the correct word for each definition.

reward	composer	expert	natural-born	honor	devil	performance

1 something that you are given because of good work: _____

2 an act of playing music, acting, or dancing: _____

3 showing a talent without having to learn it: _____

4 something that shows other people respect you: _____

5 someone who writes music to be played by a musician: _____

6 someone who has a high level of skill or knowledge in something: _____

• Before Reading   Have you ever wondered why standardization is important?

Reading 1

When you go to the store for a light bulb, you know the bulb will fit in your lamp. When you buy a camera battery, you don't have to worry that it will be too big or too small for your camera. You will easily find the wheel for your bicycle when you need to replace it. All of these things are 5 made possible by standards, although we don't often think about them.

In the 1800s, many new technologies developed. However, they weren't standardized, and this caused many problems. _____(A)_____, early railroad tracks were not 10 the same size. ⓐ Many people hoped to cross the country by train. ⓑ Some were wider than others. ⓒ Because of this, trains had a difficult time traveling long distances. ⓓ In America, the equipment used to fight fires was not standardized either. During a big fire in Baltimore, firefighters from other cities came to help. But they couldn't fit their hoses to Baltimore's equipment. Each hose was a different size! 15

People decided they needed standards to improve trade and public safety. In 1947, the International Organization for Standardization (ISO) was created. The ISO works with the world's
20 countries to make sure standards are followed. So the next time you buy a light bulb and it fits in your lamp, thank the ISO.

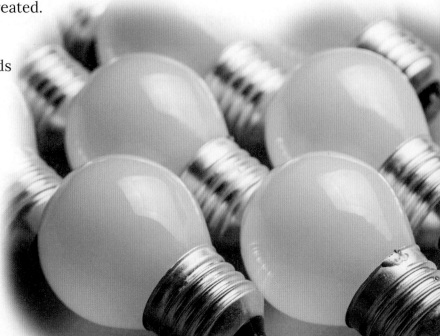

1 **What is the best title for the passage?**

① How to Choose Good Products

② Funny Mistakes Made by the ISO

③ The Importance of Standardization

④ The Problems of Different Standards

2 **What is the main point of the 1st paragraph?**

① Standards are a big part of our everyday lives.

② There are too many kinds of products these days.

③ People should be more careful when buying things.

④ It is a good idea to make a list before you go shopping.

3 **What is the best choice for blank (A)?**

① As a result

② In addition

③ For example

④ On the other hand

4 **Which sentence is NOT needed in the passage?**

① ⓐ   ② ⓑ   ③ ⓒ   ④ ⓓ

5 **The ISO was created in 1947 because people thought standards could _____ .**

6 **The underlined sentence tells us that _____ .**

① we should pay for what the ISO does

② light bulbs produced by the ISO are safer

③ we know little about why the ISO was created

④ the ISO develops standards to make our lives easier

The International Organization for Standardization is called the ISO for short. (ⓐ) But why are the letters of the acronym "ISO" and not "IOS" as you'd expect? (ⓑ) It's because the organization found out that the letters for "International Organization for Standardization" would be different in different languages. (ⓒ) So the organization's founders decided to choose an ⁵ all-purpose name that would be—you guessed it—standard across all countries! (ⓓ) They chose "ISO," from the Greek word "*isos*," meaning "equal." (ⓔ) So whatever country you're in, the acronym of the organization is always ISO.

Where would the following sentence best fit?

> For example, it would be "IOS" in English and "OIN (Organisation Internationale de Normalisation)" in French.

① ⓐ   ② ⓑ   ③ ⓒ   ④ ⓓ   ⑤ ⓔ

Summary / Graphic Organizer

A Choose the correct words to fill in the blanks.

| tracks size creation wheel standardization languages equipment |

Reading 1

Cause

problems without _____

• Example 1: Trains could not travel on _____ of different sizes.

• Example 2: Firefighters couldn't use each other's _____ .

▼

Effect

The _____ of the International Organization for Standardization

→ People can use products without worrying if they're the right _____ .

Reading 2

The International Organization of Standardization chose to use "ISO" for its acronym because they wanted it to be standard for all countries and _____ .

Vocabulary

B Complete each sentence with the best word.

| equipment developed fit distance trade standard founder |

1 The book was too big to _____ in her bag.

2 A scanner is a useful piece of _____ for the office.

3 I can't believe he went such a long _____ in only one hour!

4 _____ between the two countries has decreased due to the war.

5 The place has quickly _____ from a small town into a big city.

6 The _____ of length in France is the meter.

UNIT 17 People

• Before Reading   Do you have anything that you enjoy doing with your father?

Reading 1

Have you heard about Team Hoyt? Its members were Dick Hoyt and his son Rick. Together, they joined many marathon races and other competitions. What's surprising is that Rick, now in his 60s, has been unable to walk or talk since birth.

Rick has been in a wheelchair all his life because of a serious medical condition. Since the age of 11, he has been able to communicate with others through a computer. One day he told his dad he wanted to take part in a five-mile run. But how would he be able to do it? Dick looked for ways to realize his son's dream and finally thought up an idea how they could run the race together. During the race, Dick ran and pushed Rick in his wheelchair. They finished behind most of the other runners, but Rick felt something special during the race. He didn't feel handicapped anymore!

This experience changed both Rick and his family forever. ⓐThe father-and-son team began racing more and more often. ⓑControlled breathing is important for marathons. ⓒThough hard and full of difficulties, all the challenges have been worth it. ⓓMore than that, the story of Team Hoyt has touched and encouraged many around the world and shown that people with disabilities can lead normal lives.

1 What is the best title for the passage?

① Going Beyond Disability

② Running Improves Your Life

③ What Makes Marathons Special

④ The Importance of Loving Your Family

2 Rick has been unable to talk since birth, but he can communicate

_____ .

3 From the underlined part in the 2nd paragraph, we learn about

_____ .

① Dick's ability to win races

② Dick's great love for his son

③ Rick's passion for his dream

④ Rick's worry about big challenges

4 Which sentence is NOT needed in the passage?

① ⓐ   ② ⓑ   ③ ⓒ   ④ ⓓ

5 According to the passage, how do the Hoyts affect other people?

① They encourage people to finish a full marathon.

② They show that participating in sports can improve your health.

③ They make governments focus on the needs of disabled people.

④ They teach that many things are possible in spite of one's disabilities.

6 What is NOT true according to the passage?

① Team Hoyt was a father and a son.

② Rick has been disabled from birth.

③ Rick forgot his disability during the races.

④ Team Hoyt is famous for winning several races.

Here's an interview with a member of Team Hoyt—Rick Hoyt.

Q Did you ever think you could become an athlete?

A When I was born, the doctors told my parents that my brain couldn't communicate with my muscles. They even told my dad to forget about my future. But my parents believed I was a special boy with a bright future ahead of me. Because of their support, I thought I could do anything.   5

Q Why did you and your father participate in such hard sports?

A One reason is that we loved it! But that's not the only reason. We really hoped that through our achievements, we could show that I am just like everybody else.

Q _____

A Sure. In the early days, nobody wanted to talk to us. Some people didn't even want us   10
to compete, and they were quite cold towards us. Finally, people realized how great we were and how much I was enjoying myself.

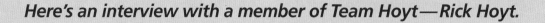

What is the best choice for the blank?

① How much did you exercise before a race?

② How was your last race with your father, Dick Hoyt?

③ Did you ever imagine Team Hoyt would be so famous?

④ What would you like to tell those who want a challenge?

⑤ Have you ever experienced any difficulties during the races?

Summary / Graphic Organizer

A Choose the correct words to fill in the blanks.

finish	disabilities	competing	wheelchair	come true

Reading 1

Dick Hoyt and his son Rick called themselves Team Hoyt when they participated in races. The main difference between the Hoyts and other runners was that Rick was in a _____. One day, Rick told Dick he wanted to participate in a race. To make his son's dream _____, Dick pushed Rick in his wheelchair while he ran. They were one of the last teams to _____ the race, but Rick was very happy. After that race, Team Hoyt started _____ in marathons and many other races.

Vocabulary

B Choose the correct word for each definition.

serious	competition	realize	birth	challenge	passion	athlete

1 something new and difficult which needs great effort: _____

2 to make your thoughts or ideas actually happen: _____

3 bad or dangerous enough to make you worried: _____

4 a powerful emotion or feeling: _____

5 a person who plays one or multiple sports well: _____

6 an event where people try to be the best at something: _____

Reading 1

Many people think that only humans use tools. However, some animals use objects in their environment as tools. Sea otters, for example, use rocks as tools. When a sea otter finds a hard shell with a tasty sea creature inside, it looks for a big rock. Then the otter hits the hard shell on ⁵ the rock. The shell opens up and the otter eats the creature inside.

Chimpanzees also use tools. They use a stick to catch termites. (ⓐ) Because termites live inside mounds, chimps can't catch them by hand. (ⓑ) So, a chimp finds ¹⁰ a branch and pulls off its leaves and side branches. (ⓒ) Then it breaks the stick to the perfect size. (ⓓ) When the chimp pulls the branch back out, it can enjoy the tasty termites that stick to it.

Scientists wanted to know more about how animals use tools. So, they put naked mole-rats in plastic tubes. The mole-rats chewed holes in the plastic to ¹⁵ get out. Interestingly, they placed little pieces of wood behind their front teeth before they chewed. These "dust masks" kept plastic dust out of their throats. How is such
_____(A)_____ possible? Is it intelligence or instinct?
²⁰ Scientists hope to find the answer someday.

76

1 **What is the main idea of the passage?**

① Some animals use objects as tools.

② Where animals live affects what they eat.

③ Some animals can learn human behavior.

④ Animals are good at finding their favorite food.

2 **According to the passage, what is true about sea otters?**

① They enjoy eating the shells of sea creatures.

② They search for shellfish by throwing rocks.

③ They always carry tools for their meals.

④ They use large rocks to eat creatures covered with shells.

3 **Where would the following sentence best fit?**

It then carefully puts it into a hole in the termite mound.

① ⓐ   ② ⓑ   ③ ⓒ   ④ ⓓ

4 **Why did naked mole-rats use dust masks?**

_____

5 **What is the best choice for blank (A)?**

① strength

② difficulty

③ creativity

④ communication

6 **How does the writer develop the topic in the passage?**

① by questioning well-known ideas

② by giving examples of animals using tools

③ by describing how animals use their hands

④ by introducing research about animals' habits

How can we know if some animals are true inventors or not? How can we explain their behavior? Since we can't ask them, scientists try to answer this question by watching them. If the use of tools were an inborn ability, most chimps, for example, would use a stick in the same way. However, each chimp makes and uses tools differently. In addition, young chimps learn their skills ⁵ by watching older chimps. The first few times, they cannot make tools well. However, young chimps get better at making tools as they grow up. All these facts show us that some animals are inventive.

To summarize the passage, what is the best choice for blanks (A) and (B)?

> By watching the behavior of animals, scientists have learned that some animals are _____(A)_____ and can use _____(B)_____ in different ways.

	(A)		(B)
①	observers	—	skills
②	inventors	—	tools
③	inventors	—	skills
④	scientists	—	tools
⑤	scientists	—	inventions

Summary / Graphic Organizer

A Choose the correct words to fill in the blanks.

protect	invent	open	intelligence	tools

Reading 1

Humans aren't the only ones who use tools. Some animals make their own _____ too. Sea otters, for example, use rocks to _____ shells so they can eat what's inside. Chimpanzees put branches into termite holes and then eat the termites on them. And naked mole-rats know how to _____ their throats from dust by using little pieces of wood. Scientists aren't sure if this kind of behavior is caused by instinct or _____, but they want to find out.

Vocabulary

B Complete each sentence with the best word.

inborn	behavior	tool	chew	sticking	inventor	shell

1 The peanut butter kept _____ to the roof of his mouth.

2 Some people argue that children have a(n) _____ ability to learn language.

3 If I had the right _____, I could finish the work sooner.

4 Leonardo da Vinci was a famous painter and _____.

5 Everyone agreed that his _____ at the restaurant was wrong.

6 You should _____ your food well before you swallow it.

Reading 1

The day was December 1, 1955. Rosa Parks, an African-American, got on a city bus in Montgomery, Alabama, and took a seat right in front. ⓐAll the people on the bus were surprised. ⓑIn Alabama at that time, African-Americans had to sit at the back of the bus. ⓒMost people used to ride a bus rather than driving their car. ⓓFront seats were for whites only. The bus driver angrily told Parks that she should give up her seat, but she refused. She believed that people of every race should have the same rights. This act turned Rosa Parks into the "_____(A)_____."

Parks was taken by the police and put in jail. Her trial lasted more than a year. During the trial, most African-Americans in Montgomery didn't ride the city buses. It was a protest. In addition to the rules about bus seats, they were protesting many other unfair laws in Alabama. _____(B)_____, black children were not allowed to ride on school buses.

Finally, the trial ended. The US Supreme Court decided it was unfair to have separate seats for whites and blacks on city buses. This was an important victory for the civil rights movement, and it was thanks to Rosa Parks.

1 **What is the best choice for blank (A)?**

① Founder of the Bus Safety Laws

② Leader of the American Women's Society

③ Woman Who Brought the Rich and Poor Together

④ Mother of the Modern-Day Civil Rights Movement

2 **Which sentence is NOT needed in the passage?**

① ⓐ   ② ⓑ   ③ ⓒ   ④ ⓓ

3 **What was the rule for African-Americans on buses in Alabama in the 1950s?**

_____

4 **What is the best choice for blank (B)?**

① However

② Otherwise

③ Therefore

④ For example

5 **Why was Rosa Parks' act important?**

① She stood up for equal rights of all African-Americans.

② She was the first African-American woman to win a trial.

③ She changed laws that were bad for women and children.

④ She started a movement for African-American children's rights.

6 **What is the best word to describe Rosa Parks?**

① shy

② polite

③ ordinary

④ brave

From 1876 to 1965, there were laws in some parts of America
_____. These were known as the Jim Crow
laws. Because of these laws, there were "Whites Only" signs in many schools,
restaurants, theaters, and hotels. The places that non-whites could use were
marked with "Colored" signs. The seats on some trains and buses were also ⁵
divided by race. Even marriages between white and non-white people were not
allowed in many states. Fortunately, these laws were finally ended by the Civil
Rights Act of 1964.

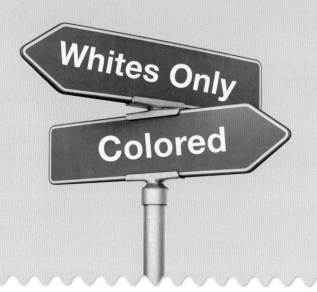

What is the best choice for the blank?

① to protect non-white people from white people

② to encourage Americans to live where they were born

③ to stop non-white people from going to private places

④ to build more equal communities regardless of people's skin color

⑤ to keep white people separated from non-white people in public places

Summary / Graphic Organizer

A Choose the correct words to fill in the blanks.

ride	white	laws	black	separate	protest

Reading 1

Rosa Parks' act: She sat in a bus seat that was for _____ people only.

▼

African-American _____:

They refused to _____ the city buses.

▼

The US Supreme Court's decision:

It is not fair to have _____ seats for black people.

Reading 2

Until the Civil Rights Act, many American states had _____ to keep white people and non-white people separated.

Vocabulary

B Choose the correct word for each definition.

separate	trial	protest	allow	law	last	mark

1 to let someone do or have something: _____

2 a system of rules that everyone in a country or society must follow: _____

3 a legal process to judge whether someone is guilty or not: _____

4 a statement or action showing public disagreement: _____

5 to move apart or divide into parts or groups: _____

6 to write a symbol to show something: _____

Reading 1

The Nazca Lines are a series of giant drawings in the Nazca Desert in Peru. It is believed that they were drawn between 200 BC and 600 AD. The lines include 300 figures such as birds, spiders, monkeys, and *geometric shapes. The drawings are so huge that they can only be seen clearly 5 from the air. So, it's surprising that ancient people could draw these figures on the ground without flying skills. Moreover, it's hard to believe that these drawings have lasted for thousands of years.

Since their discovery in the 1920s, people have tried 10 to find out what these lines were drawn for. Some people suggest the lines were created for religious reasons. The lines and shapes may have been made for the gods the Nazcans worshipped. (ⓐ) By making large drawings, the Nazcan people hoped that gods in the sky could see the figures. (ⓑ) On the other hand, some say the lines were a giant calendar. (ⓒ) Some people even suggest that the lines were 15 drawn by aliens as a runway for spaceships. (ⓓ) But it seems that none of these can explain the lines clearly. After thousands of years, this important artwork is still _____(A)_____ .

*geometric shape: a basic shape, such as a square, a circle, or a triangle

1 **What is the passage mainly about?**

① artistic cities of Peru

② ancient Peruvian events

③ puzzling artwork in Peru

④ the artwork of South America

2 **What is NOT mentioned about the Nazca Lines?**

① where they were found

② when they were made

③ what they look like

④ who first found them

3 **Why are the Nazca Lines surprising? (Choose two.)**

① because they are so big

② because they look like real animals

③ because it took so long to finish them

④ because they have lasted a long time

4 **Where would the following sentence best fit?**

> They believe the figures are related to the stars and the change of the seasons.

① ⓐ   ② ⓑ   ③ ⓒ   ④ ⓓ

5 **What is NOT suggested as a purpose of the Nazca Lines?**

① They were drawn to worship the gods of the Nazcan people.

② They were used as a giant ancient calendar.

③ They were drawn to show the power of Nazcan people.

④ They were created by aliens to be used as a runway.

6 **What is the best choice for blank (A)?**

① a pleasure   ② a discovery   ③ a problem   ④ a mystery

Maria Reiche was an archaeologist who spent her life studying the amazing Nazca Lines. Although she was born in Germany, she lived in Peru for most of her life. There she had a chance to see the Nazca Lines and became very interested in them. For about forty years, Maria studied the wonderful Nazca Lines and tried to protect them. ⓐ Unfortunately, the people of Peru were not ₅ aware of their importance as a heritage. ⓑ The government of Peru even built a highway across one of the drawings! ⓒ This highway is part of the Pan-American Highway, and it connects most of the countries in South America. ⓓ Eventually, Maria persuaded the government of Peru to stop people from damaging them. ⓔ Thanks to her efforts, UNESCO declared the Nazca Lines a World Heritage ₁₀ Site in 1994.

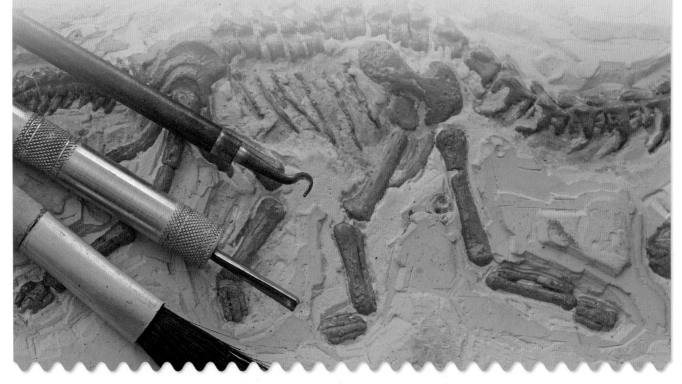

Which sentence is NOT needed in the passage?

① ⓐ   ② ⓑ   ③ ⓒ   ④ ⓓ   ⑤ ⓔ

Summary / Graphic Organizer

A   Choose the correct words to fill in the blanks.

spaceships   calendar   mystery   shape   archaeologist   religious

Reading 1

Nazca Lines

• giant drawings in Peru

• huge and very old

Possible purposes

1. created for _____ reasons

2. used as a giant _____

3. drawn by aliens as a runway for _____

▼

still a(n) _____

Reading 2

Maria Reiche was a German _____ who studied and protected the Nazca Lines in Peru, and her efforts helped them to become a World Heritage Site in 1994.

Vocabulary

B   Complete each sentence with the best word.

discovery   suggest   figures   effort   religious   worship   persuade

1   In Islam, people don't eat pork for _____ reasons.

2   We're making a special _____ to finish the project on time.

3   The _____ of DNA was a very important event in the history of science.

4   In the past, Egyptians used to _____ the sun as their god.

5   The child loved to draw animal _____ with his crayons.

6   I tried to _____ her to come to my birthday party.

Photo credits

www.shutterstock.com

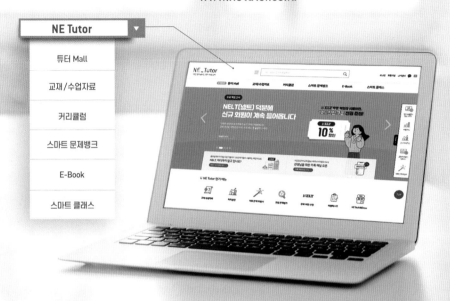

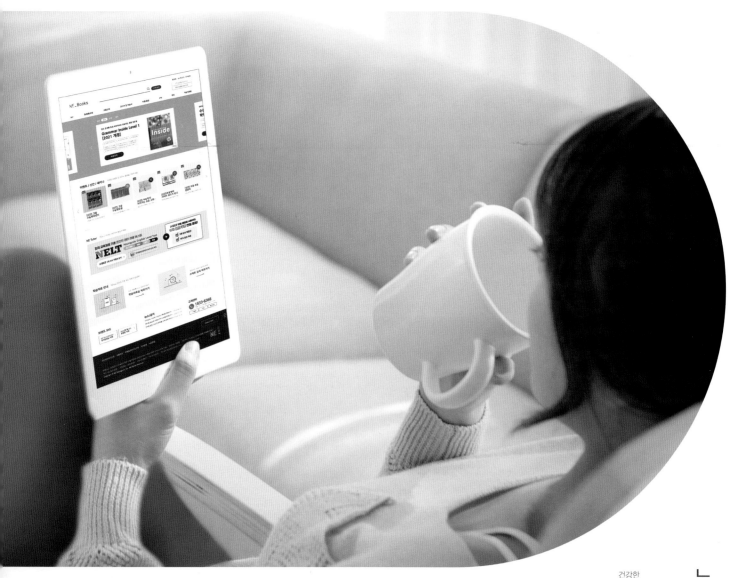

JUNIOR
READING EXPERT

A Theme-Based Reading Course for Young EFL Learners

Level **3**

Word Book

UNIT 01 The Environment

prime minister	몡 총리
pick up	줍다
trash	몡 쓰레기
post	동 게시하다
last	동 계속되다
be made up of	~로 구성되다
phrase	몡 어구
act	몡 행위
necessary	혱 필수적인
notice	동 알아차리다, 발견하다
habit	몡 습관
daily	혱 매일의
daily routine	일과
movement	몡 (사람들이 조직적으로 벌이는) 운동
spread	동 퍼지다
global	혱 세계적인
search	몡 검색
give it a try	시도하다, 한번 해보다
build	동 짓다; 형성하다
environmental	혱 환경의
environment	몡 환경
issue	몡 문제

meaningful	형 의미 있는
opinion	명 의견
enable	동 ~할 수 있게 하다
participate in	~에 참여하다
empty	동 비우다
neighborhood	명 동네
save	동 구하다
consider	동 고려하다
exciting	형 신나는, 흥미진진한
free	형 자유로운; 무료의; ~이 없는
event	명 행사
throw away	버리다
reuse	동 재사용하다
metal	형 금속의
straw	명 빨대
healthy	형 건강한
ocean	명 바다
community	명 지역 사회
reduce	동 줄이다
waste	명 쓰레기
volunteer	명 자원봉사자
gather	동 모으다
delicious	형 맛있는
campaign	명 캠페인

| celebrate | 동 기념하다, 축하하다 |
| planet | 명 행성; 세상 |

UNIT 02 *Society*

stay up late	늦게까지 자지 않고 있다
presentation	명 발표
barely	부 거의 ~ 아니게
used to-v	(과거에) ~이었다[했었다]
lately	부 최근에
depressed	형 우울한
depression	명 우울증
burnout	명 번아웃, 극도의 피로
burn out	에너지를 다 써버리다
syndrome	명 증후군
experience	동 경험하다
stress out	스트레스를 주다
closely	부 밀접하게
report	동 알리다
irregular	형 불규칙적인
at risk	위험에 처한
employee	명 직원, 근로자
motivate	동 동기를 부여하다

trust	통 신뢰하다, 믿다
identify	통 확인하다; 찾다, 발견하다
sign	명 징후, 징조
condition	명 상태; 질환
communication	명 의사소통
support	명 지지, 도움
symptom	명 증상
overcome	통 극복하다
dissatisfaction	명 불만족
salary	명 급여
competition	명 경쟁
examine	통 진찰하다, 검사하다
session	명 기간, 시간
prevent	통 막다, 예방하다
task	명 일, 과제
order	명 순서
importance	명 중요성
level	명 정도, 수준
productive	형 생산하는; 생산적인
guilty	형 죄책감이 드는

UNIT 03 *Origins*

Ferris wheel	대관람차
ride	(명) (놀이공원 등에 있는) 놀이 기구 (동) 타다
amusement park	놀이공원
upright	(형) 수직으로 세워 둔
passenger car	객차
edge	(명) 끝, 가장자리, 모서리
rotate	(동) 회전하다
invent	(동) 발명하다
invention	(명) 발명
engineer	(명) 엔지니어
amazing	(형) 놀라운
fair	(명) 박람회
impressive	(형) 인상적인
original	(형) 원래의, 최초의
at once	한 번에
operate	(동) 운영하다
recycle	(동) 재활용하다
battleship	(명) 전함
inspire	(동) 영감을 주다
similar	(형) 비슷한
carnival	(명) 카니발, 축제
beat	(동) 이기다; 더 낫다, 능가하다

success	명 성공
weight	명 무게
material	명 재료
shut down	(공장, 가게의) 문을 닫다
cost	명 비용
design	동 설계하다
introduce	동 소개하다
bring	동 가져오다
joy	명 즐거움
found	동 설립하다
attract	동 끌어들이다
proper	형 적절한, 제대로 된
discover	동 발견하다
spring	명 샘
visit	동 방문하다
entertainer	명 연예인
salesman	명 판매원
fame	명 명성
power	동 동력을 공급하다, 작동시키다
electricity	명 전기

UNIT 04 *Sports*

professional	몡 프로 혱 전문적인
referee	몡 (축구, 권투 등의) 심판
league	몡 (스포츠 경기의) 리그, 연맹
make sure	확실하게 하다
break	툥 깨뜨리다; (규칙 등을) 어기다
penalty	몡 벌칙
decision	몡 결정
yell at	~에게 소리지르다
attack	툥 공격하다
fit	혱 건강한
throughout	쩐 ~ 내내
whole	혱 전체의
unexpected	혱 예기치 않은
national	혱 국가의; 전국적인
origin	몡 기원
relaxed	혱 편안한
satisfied	혱 만족한
uninterested	혱 무관심한
at least	적어도, 최소한
tool	몡 도구
whistle	몡 호루라기
foul	몡 반칙, 파울

goal	(명) 골, 골문
score	(동) 득점을 하다
keep track of	~을 놓치지 않고 따라가다
injury	(명) 부상
injured	(형) 부상을 입은
warn	(동) 경고하다
throw out of	퇴장시키다, 쫓아내다
flip	(동) (손가락으로) 튀기다, 휙 던지다
defend	(동) 방어하다
assistant	(명) 조수 (형) 보조의

UNIT 05 · *Health*

let out	~을 내다[유출하다]
burp	(명) 트림 (동) 트림을 하다
probably	(부) 아마
scold	(동) 꾸짖다
rude	(형) 무례한
exactly	(부) 정확히
escape	(동) 탈출하다
stomach	(명) 위
muscle	(명) 근육
throat	(명) 목구멍

8

rush	동 돌진하다
swallow	동 삼키다
liter	명 리터
normal	형 정상적인
polite	형 예의 바른
appreciation	명 감사
embarrassing	형 당황케 하는
at the same time	동시에
soda	명 탄산음료
bubble	명 거품, 기포
manner	명 (~s) 예의범절, 예절
table manner	식사예절
think of A as B	A를 B로 여기다
methane	명 메탄
per	전 ~당, ~마다
increase	동 증가시키다
global warming	지구 온난화
produce	동 생산하다
cause	동 일으키다, 야기하다
diet	명 식단, 먹이

regular	혱 규칙적인; 일반적인
be interested in	~에 관심이 있다
historical site	유적지
historical	혱 역사적, 역사상의
site	명 위치, 장소
terrible	혱 끔찍한
vacation	명 방학; 휴가
prison	명 교도소, 감옥
prisoner	명 죄수
prison guard	교도관
military	혱 군사의
guest	명 손님; 투숙객
treat	동 대(우)하다, 취급하다
employee	명 종업원, 고용인
punish	동 처벌하다, 벌주다
museum	명 박물관
political	혱 정치적인
former	혱 과거의, 이전의
cell	명 감방
educational	혱 교육의, 교육적인
scary	혱 무서운, 겁나는
relieved	혱 안도하는, 다행으로 여기는

rule	통 통치하다, 지배하다
personal	형 개인의, 개인적인
extremely	부 극도로
memorial	명 기념비
attack	명 공격
directly	부 곧장, 직접적으로
affect	통 영향을 끼치다
policy	명 정책, 방침
reschedule	통 일정을 변경하다
refund	명 환불(금)
available	형 구할[이용할] 수 있는
on time	시간에 맞추어서

UNIT 07 Teens

nervous	형 긴장한, 떨리는
cheek	명 볼, 뺨
bright	형 밝은, 선명한
shy	형 수줍은
shyness	명 수줍음
first of all	우선
comfortable	형 편안한
situation	명 상황

overcome	⑧ 극복하다
continue	⑧ 계속되다
memorize	⑧ 암기하다
at least	적어도
blame	⑧ 비난하다
breath	⑲ 숨, 호흡
encourage	⑧ 격려하다
immediately	⑨ 즉시
unique	⑲ 독특한, 고유의
deal with	(문제, 과제 등을) 처리하다, 해결하다
anger	⑲ 화, 분노
annoy	⑧ 짜증나게 하다
greeting	⑲ (~s) 인사말
calm down	진정하다
mad	⑲ 미친; 몹시 화가 난
step onto	~에 올라서다
trip	⑧ (발이) 걸리다, 헛디디다
blush	⑧ 얼굴을 붉히다
embarrassed	⑲ 당황스러운, 당황한
embarrassment	⑲ 당혹감
chemical	⑲ 화학물질
widen	⑧ ~의 폭을 넓히다
blood vessel	혈관
flow	⑧ 흐르다

| common | 휑 흔한 |
| confident | 휑 자신감 있는 |

UNIT 08 *Literature*

Jewish	휑 유대인의
Jew	몡 유대인
take over	탈취[장악]하다
force	통 강요하다
hide	통 숨다
recently	뷔 최근에
horrible	휑 끔찍한
protector	몡 보호자
agree	통 동의하다
reject	통 거부하다
relative	몡 친척
dentist	몡 치과의사
currently	뷔 현재
gentleman	몡 신사
behave	통 처신[행동]하다
politely	뷔 공손히, 예의 바르게
fit in	어울리다, 맞다
tool	몡 기구, 도구

take care of	~을 돌보다
lately	(부) 최근에
accept	(동) 받아들이다
up to	~까지
journal	(명) 일기
be in danger	위험에 처하다
describe	(동) 묘사하다, 기술하다
talkative	(형) 말하기를 좋아하는, 수다스러운
unlike	(전) ~와 달리
death	(명) 죽음
publish	(동) 출판하다

UNIT 09 Issues

hate	(동) 싫어하다
technological	(형) 기술적인
technology	(명) 기술
advancement	(명) 진보
grocery	(명) 식료품
select	(동) 선택하다
scan	(동) 스캔하다
support	(동) 지지하다
check out	계산하다

accuracy	몡 정확성
accurate	휑 정확한
order	몡 주문
exactly	틧 정확히
employer	몡 고용주
benefit	동 이익을 얻다 몡 혜택, 이득
customer	몡 고객
oppose	동 반대하다
frustrated	휑 좌절감을 느끼는, 불만스러워 하는
cashier	몡 계산원
skilled	휑 숙련된
efficiently	틧 효율적으로
bag	동 봉지[가방 등]에 넣다
consider	동 고려하다
various	휑 다양한
need	몡 (~s) 요구
communicate	동 의사소통하다
refuse	동 거부하다
ability	몡 능력
gap	몡 차이
digital divide	정보 격차
term	몡 용어
include	동 포함하다
financial	휑 금융[재정]의

technical	형 기술적인
exist	동 존재하다
developed country	선진국
underdeveloped country	개발도상국
educated	형 교육 받은
uneducated	형 교육 받지 못한
available	형 이용 가능한
limited	형 제한된, 한정된
access	명 접근
option	명 선택권
increase	명 증가
education	명 교육
lack	동 ~이 없다, 부족하다
resource	명 자원
develop	동 개발시키다
obviously	부 분명히
issue	명 문제
knowledge	명 지식

UNIT 10 Jobs

normal	형 보통의
run	동 달리다; 운영하다

nonprofit	형 비영리의
organization	명 단체, 기구
equipment	명 장비
facility	명 (~ies) 시설
care	명 걱정; 치료
area	명 지역
treat	동 대하다; 치료하다
million	명 100만
worthwhile	형 가치 있는
volunteer	명 자원봉사자 동 자원하다
free	형 자유로운; 무료의
medical	형 의학적인
local	형 현지의, 그 지역의
disease	명 질병
short-term	형 단기간의
long-term	형 장기간의
challenging	형 도전적인
meaningful	형 의미 있는, 중요한
amnesty	명 사면
border	명 국경
disaster	명 재난
similar	형 비슷한
environment	명 환경
protect	동 보호하다

human right	인권
well-known	형 유명한, 잘 알려진
stand for	~을 의미하다
non-governmental	형 비정부의

UNIT 11 *Food*

neighborhood	명 동네, 이웃
flavor	명 맛, 풍미
shape	명 모양
choice	명 선택, 선택지
troublesome	형 성가신, 골치 아픈
complain	동 불평하다
teach a lesson	~에게 훈계하다
slice	동 얇게 썰다
peel	동 ~의 껍질을 벗기다
store	동 저장하다
wooden	형 나무로 된
barrel	명 (목재, 금속으로 된) 통
machine	명 기계
mass-produce	동 대량 생산하다
wax-coated	형 왁스를 바른
serve	동 (음식을) 제공하다, 차려내다

regret	몡 후회
disappointment	몡 실망
by chance	우연히
taste	동 ~의 맛이 나다
thus	부 그러므로, 따라서
meat	몡 고기
couch	몡 소파
idiom	몡 관용구
contain	동 포함하다
origin	몡 기원
traditional	형 전통적인
recipe	몡 조리법
dish	몡 접시; 요리
joke	몡 농담

UNIT 12 *Science*

spider web	거미줄(집)
closet	몡 옷장, 벽장
ceiling	몡 천장
interested	형 관심 있어 하는
interest	동 흥미를 끌다
silk	몡 명주실, 비단

material	몡 물질
bend	통 구부리다
stretch	통 늘이다
steel	몡 강철
product	몡 제품
produce	통 생산하다
bullet	몡 총탄
airbag	몡 (자동차의) 에어백
harmful	혱 해로운; 위험한
harm	통 해치다
passenger	몡 승객
cut	몡 베인 상처
heal	통 (상처, 병 등을) 고치다; 낫다
collect	통 모으다
strength	몡 힘
emphasize	통 강조하다
injury	몡 부상
dislike	통 싫어하다
second thought	재고(다시 생각함)
insect	몡 곤충
including	젼 ~을 포함하여
venom	몡 (독사 등의) 독액
poison	몡 독, 독물
crop	몡 (농)작물

hurt	동 다치게 하다, 아픔을 주다
natural	형 천연의
bother	동 괴롭히다

UNIT 13 *Culture*

noisy	형 소란스러운
parade	명 퍼레이드, 행진
clover	명 클로버, 토끼풀
suddenly	부 갑자기
pinch	동 꼬집다
celebrate	동 축하하다, 기념하다
holy	형 성스러운
slave	명 노예
Ireland	명 아일랜드
Irish	형 아일랜드의
escape	동 탈출하다
priest	명 성직자
rest	명 나머지; 휴식
spread	동 퍼뜨리다, 전파하다
Christianity	명 기독교
legend	명 전설
symbol	명 상징

costume	몡 복장
competition	몡 경쟁; 시합
environmental	혱 환경의
in memory of	~의 기념으로
touching	혱 감동적인
yummy	혱 맛있는
go on	계속되다
surprise	몡 뜻밖의 선물
guest	몡 초대손님
bottom	몡 밑바닥
host	동 주최하다, 진행하다

 # *Technology*

response	몡 응답
typically	뿐 일반적으로
share	동 공유하다
be similar to	~와 비슷하다
barcode	몡 바코드
scan	동 스캔하다
dot	몡 점
advertisement	몡 광고
reader	몡 판독기

identify	동 인식하다
section	명 부분
examine	동 검사하다
recognize	동 인식하다
measure	동 측정하다
reflect	동 반사하다
absorb	동 흡수하다
access	동 접근하다 명 접근
incredibly	부 믿을 수 없을 정도로, 엄청나게
convenient	형 편리한
solution	명 해결책
detail	명 세부 정보
instruction manual	사용 설명서
package	명 포장
industry	명 산업
rival	명 경쟁자
effective	형 효과적인
be composed of	~로 구성되다
function	동 기능하다
part	명 일부; 부품
keep track of	~을 기록하다; 추적하다
production	명 생산
limiting	형 제한하는
purpose	명 목적

up to	~까지
create	동 창조[창작]하다
own	동 소유하다
right	명 권리, (~s) 소유권(지적 재산권)
decide	동 결정하다
freely	부 자유롭게
replace A with B	A를 B로 대체하다

The Arts

instrument	명 도구; 악기
worth	형 ~의 가치가 있는
cannon	명 대포
talented	형 재능 있는
take care of	~을 돌보다
city hall	시청
expert	명 전문가
care for	~을 돌보다, 관리하다
repair	동 수리하다
necessary	형 필수적인
top	명 꼭대기 형 최고의
condition	명 상태
time	명 시간; 시대

showcase	몡 진열장
reward	몡 보상, 상
get to-v	~하게 되다
honor	몡 영예
musician	몡 음악가
second-most	혱 두 번째로 가장 많은
give a concert	연주회를 열다
soul	몡 영혼
devil	몡 악마
according to	~에 따르면
researcher	몡 연구원
natural-born	혱 타고난
composer	몡 작곡가
as well	《문장의 끝에서》 ~도 역시
performance	몡 공연
work	몡 일; 작품
mysterious	혱 기이한, 신비로운
talent	몡 재능

UNIT 16 *The Economy*

light bulb	몡 전구
fit	동 (꼭) 맞다; 끼워 맞추다, 끼우다

wheel	몡 바퀴
standard	몡 표준
standardize	통 표준화하다
standardization	몡 표준화
develop	통 발전하다
cause	통 유발하다
railroad track	철로
cross	통 (길, 사막 등을) 가로지르다
distance	몡 거리
equipment	몡 장비
hose	몡 (물을 끄는) 호스, 수도용 관
improve	통 향상시키다
trade	몡 거래, 무역
public	혱 공공의, 공중의
organization	몡 기구, 조직
for short	줄여서
letter	몡 (알파벳의) 철자, 글자
acronym	몡 두음어 (몇 개 단어의 머리글자로 된 단어)
founder	몡 창설자
all-purpose	혱 만능의, 다목적의
equal	혱 동등한

People

marathon	몡 마라톤
competition	몡 경쟁; 경기
birth	몡 출생
serious	혱 심각한
medical	혱 의학의
medical condition	질병
communicate	동 의사소통하다
take part in	~에 참가하다
run	몡 달리기, 경주
look for	~을 찾다
realize	동 실현하다; 깨닫다
finally	튀 드디어, 마침내
think up	~을 생각해 내다
handicapped	혱 장애를 가진
controlled	혱 조절된
breathing	몡 호흡
challenge	몡 도전
worth	혱 ~할 가치가 있는
touch	동 만지다; 감동시키다
encourage	동 격려하다, 용기를 북돋우다
disability	몡 장애
disabled	혱 장애를 가진

normal	형 보통의
beyond	전 ~을 넘어서
passion	명 열정
affect	동 ~에 영향을 미치다
participate in	~에 참가하다
focus on	~에 집중하다
athlete	명 운동선수
muscle	명 근육
ahead of	~ 앞에
achievement	명 업적
compete	동 경쟁하다, (경기에) 참가하다
cold	형 추운; 냉담한
towards	전 ~을 향해

UNIT 18 Animals

tool	명 도구
object	명 물건, 물체
sea otter	해달
shell	명 (조개 등의) 껍데기
tasty	형 맛있는
creature	명 생물
chimpanzee	명 침팬지 (= chimp)

stick	뗑 막대기 뗑 (to) ~에 달라붙다
termite	뗑 흰개미
mound	뗑 흙더미
branch	뗑 나뭇가지
naked mole-rat	벌거숭이두더지쥐
tube	뗑 관
chew	뗑 (상처, 구멍을) 씹어서 만들다, 씹다
get out	탈출하다, 도망치다
place	뗑 위치시키다, 두다
dust	뗑 티끌, 먼지
intelligence	뗑 지능
instinct	뗑 본능
behavior	뗑 행동
shellfish	뗑 조개
throw	뗑 던지다
question	뗑 질문하다; 이의를 제기하다
inventor	뗑 발명가
invention	뗑 발명품
inventive	뗑 발명의 재능이 있는
inborn	뗑 타고난
ability	뗑 능력, 재능
fact	뗑 사실
observer	뗑 관찰자

take a seat	앉다
seat	몡 좌석, 자리
give up	~을 포기하다[내주다]
refuse	동 거부하다
race	몡 인종
right	몡 권리
turn A into B	A를 B로 바꾸다
jail	몡 감옥, 교도소
trial	몡 재판
last	동 지속되다, 계속하다
protest	몡 항의 동 항의하다
unfair	혱 불공평한
law	몡 법, 법규
allow	동 허용하다
Supreme Court	대법원
separate	혱 분리된 동 분리시키다
victory	몡 승리
civil rights	인권, 시민권
movement	몡 움직임; (정치, 사회적) 운동
society	몡 사회; 협회
modern-day	혱 현대의
stand up for	~을 변호[옹호]하다

equal	⑧ 동등한
ordinary	⑧ 보통의, 평범한
sign	⑲ 표시, 표지판
non-white	⑲ 백인이 아닌 사람, 유색인
mark	⑧ 표시하다
colored	⑧ 유색인의
divide	⑧ 나누다
marriage	⑲ 결혼
fortunately	⑨ 다행히
private	⑧ 사적인, 사유의
community	⑲ 지역 사회
regardless of	~에 관계없이

UNIT 20 *Mysteries*

Nazca	⑲ 나스카
Nazcan	⑧ 나스카(인)의
a series of	일련의
giant	⑧ 거대한
drawing	⑲ 그림
draw	⑧ 그리다
figure	⑲ 형상; 숫자
ancient	⑧ 고대의

discovery	몡 발견
suggest	통 제안하다
religious	혱 종교적인
worship	통 숭배하다
calendar	몡 달력
alien	몡 외계인
runway	몡 활주로
spaceship	몡 우주선
artwork	몡 예술작품
artistic	혱 예술의
Peruvian	혱 페루의
puzzling	혱 당혹케 하는, 헷갈리게 하는
be related to	~에 관련되어 있다
archaeologist	몡 고고학자
unfortunately	뷔 안타깝게도
be aware of	~을 알다
heritage	몡 유산, 상속 재산
highway	몡 고속도로
persuade	통 (~하라고) 설득하다
effort	몡 노력
declare	통 선언하다

JUNIOR
READING EXPERT

A Theme-Based Reading Course for Young EFL Learners

Level **3**

Answer Key

NE Neungyule

JUNIOR
READING EXPERT

A Theme-Based Reading Course for Young EFL Learners

Answer Key

Level **3**

pp.8-9

Reading 1

Before Reading I pick up plastic bottles or cans before leaving the park.

1 ④ **2** ② **3** ④ **4** ④ **5** anyone can easily go out and pick up some trash
6 (1) T (2) F

해석

어느 날 아침, 인도 총리가 해변을 산책하는 동안 쓰레기를 줍는 것이 목격되었다. 나중에, 그는 '해변에서 플로깅. 그것은 30분 넘게 지속되었습니다.'라는 말과 함께 그것에 대해 소셜 미디어에 올렸다. 그런데 '플로깅'이 무엇일까?

'플로깅'은 영어 단어 'jogging'과 '줍다'를 뜻하는 스웨덴어 어구 'plocka upp'으로 이루어져 있다. 그것은 조깅을 하거나 빨리 걷는 동안 쓰레기를 줍는 행위이다. (그래서 쓰레기봉투는 스웨덴 사람들에게 꼭 필요한 물건이다.) 그것은 2016년 스웨덴에서 에릭 알스트롬이 출근길에 길거리에서 쓰레기를 발견했을 때 시작되었다. 그는 쓰레기를 주웠고, 이것은 습관이 되었다. 시간이 지나면서, 그는 심지어 매일 달리기를 하면서 그것을 했다! 점점 더 많은 사람들이 알스트롬의 행동을 보게 되면서, 이 운동은 스웨덴 전역으로 퍼졌다.

이제, 플로깅은 세계적인 운동인데, 사람들이 온라인과 오프라인에서 그것에 대해 이야기하기 때문이다. 소셜 미디어에서 '#plogging'을 빠르게 검색하면 사람들이 그들의 동네를 청소하는 사진 수천 장을 볼 수 있다. 왜 이 운동이 증가하고 있는지 쉽게 알 수 있는데, 누구나 쉽게 나가서 쓰레기를 주울 수 있기 때문이다. 그러니 여러분도 직접 한 번 시도해 보는 게 어떨까?

어휘

prime minister 총리   pick up 줍다   trash 몡쓰레기   post 통게시하다   last 통계속되다   be made up of ~로 구성되다   phrase 몡어구   act 몡행위   necessary 혱필수적인   notice 통알아차리다, 발견하다   habit 몡습관   daily 혱매일의 (daily routine 일과)   movement 몡(사람들이 조직적으로 벌이는) 운동   spread 통퍼지다   global 혱세계적인   search 몡검색   give it a try 시도하다, 한번 해보다   [문제] build 통짓다; *형성하다   environmental 혱환경의 (environment 몡환경)   issue 몡문제   meaningful 혱의미 있는   opinion 몡의견   enable 통~할 수 있게 하다   participate in ~에 참여하다   empty 통비우다   neighborhood 몡동네

구문 해설

1행 One morning, the Prime Minister of India **was seen** picking up trash during a walk by the beach.
- was seen: '보여지다'라는 뜻으로 'be동사 + 과거분사' 형태의 수동태 (← People saw the Prime Minister of India picking up trash ...)

12행 As **more and more** people saw Ahlström's actions, the movement spread across Sweden.
- 비교급 + and + 비교급: 점점 더 ~한

19행 **It**'s easy **to see** *why the movement is growing*, **as** anyone can easily go out and pick up some trash.

- It은 가주어이고, to see는 진주어로 '~하는 것'의 의미
- why가 이끄는 간접의문문은 동사 see의 목적어 역할을 함
- as: '~이기 때문에'라는 의미로 부사절을 이끄는 접속사

Reading 2 p.10

②

해석

당신은 환경이 걱정되지만 어떻게 그것을 보호해야 할지 모르겠는가? 전 세계에서 온 몇 가지 흥미진진한 운동들을 고려해 보아라. '플라스틱 없는 7월'은 호주에서 처음 시작되었다. 이 행사 동안, 사람들은 커피 컵과 금속 빨대와 같은 일상 용품을 재사용함으로써 플라스틱을 덜 사용하고 덜 버린다. 한 달 동안 이렇게 함으로써, 그들은 건강한 습관들을 형성하고 그들의 거리, 바다, 그리고 지역 사회를 깨끗하게 유지할 수 있다. '디스코 수프의 날'은 음식물 쓰레기를 줄이기 위한 독일의 행사이다. 슈퍼마켓, 식당, 그리고 농장에는 종종 사용되지 않은 식재료가 많이 있다. 그래서 그날, 자원봉사자들은 그 식재료를 모아서 맛있는 음식을 만들기 위해 그것을 사용한다. 이러한 캠페인들은 사람들에게 그저 쓰레기를 줄이라고 말하는 것이 아니라, 사람들이 그것을 기념하도록 한다! 지구를 보호하면서 즐기는 것만큼 좋은 것은 없다.

어휘

save 동구하다 consider 동고려하다 exciting 형신나는, 흥미진진한 free 형자유로운; 무료의; *~이 없는 event 명행사 throw away 버리다 reuse 동재사용하다 metal 형금속의 straw 명빨대 healthy 형건강한 ocean 명바다 community 명지역 사회 reduce 동줄이다 waste 명쓰레기 volunteer 명자원봉사자 gather 동모으다 delicious 형맛있는 campaign 명캠페인 celebrate 동기념하다, 축하하다 [문제] planet 명행성; *세상

구문 해설

1행 **Are** you **worried about** the environment but don't know *how to save* it?

- be worried about: ~에 대해 걱정하다
- how to-v: ~하는 방법

6행 ..., they can ⎡ build healthy habits
⎢ and
⎣ **keep their streets, oceans, and communities clean.**

- keep + 목적어 + 형용사: ~을 …하게 유지[보존]하다

Unit Review

A [Reading 1] jogging, picking up, trash, movement [Reading 2] environment

B **1** reduce **2** last **3** global **4** environment **5** opinion **6** empty

Reading 1 해석

'플로깅'이라는 단어는 영어 단어 'jogging'과 '줍다'를 의미하는 스웨덴어 어구 'plocka upp'에서 유래한다. 그것은 당신이 조깅을 하는 동안 쓰레기를 줍는 행위를 가리킨다. 플로깅에 대한 아이디어는 에릭 알스트롬이라는 스웨덴 남자로부터 나왔다. 그는 출근할 때 길에서 쓰레기를 줍기 시작했다. 얼마 지나지 않아, 그는 심지어 매일 달리기를 하면서 그것을 하기 시작했다. 이제, 플로깅 운동은 전 세계로 퍼졌고, 소셜 미디어에서 유명해졌다.

Reading 2 해석

호주의 '플라스틱 없는 7월'과 독일의 '디스코 수프의 날'에 참여하는 것처럼 사람들이 환경을 보호하는 데 도움을 줄 수 있는 많은 재미있는 방법들이 있다.

UNIT 02 Society

Reading 1

Before Reading I usually listen to music or watch videos on my smartphone.

1 ③ **2** ② **3** help workers manage their stress **4** ④ **5** ③ **6** (1) T (2) F

해석

지난주 동안, 마크는 중요한 회사 발표를 준비하며 매일 밤늦도록 깨어 있다. 그는 너무 피곤해서 눈을 거의 뜨고 있지 못한다. 그는 이 일을 좋아했었지만, 최근에는 이 일에 대해 즐기는 것이 아무것도 없다. 그는 우울해지기 시작하고 있다. 이것은 '번아웃 증후군'의 한 예이다. 많은 사람들이 매우 오랫동안 너무 열심히 일할 때 이것을 경험한다. 1970년대 중반 이후로, 과학자들은 일하는 사람들이 그들의 스트레스를 관리하도록 돕기 위해 번아웃(극도의 피로감)에 대해 연구해 오고 있다.

어느 직업이든지 스트레스를 유발할 수 있지만, 정말 사람들에게 스트레스를 주는 특정한 직업들이 있을까? 그렇다! 교사, 간호사, 그리고 경찰관과 같이 다른 사람들과 밀접하게 일하는 사람들은 자주 에너지를 다 써버린 것 같은 기분을 느낀다고 말한다. 게다가, 불규칙한 시간에 일해야 하는 직업을 가진 사람들 역시 위험하다.

그래서 근무 환경이 중요하다. 직원들이 존중받고, 동기 부여가 되고, 신뢰를 받는다고 느낄 때, 그들은 자신의 일을 더 즐긴다. 또한, 번아웃의 징후를 발견할 수 있는 상사는 그것을 가진 사람들을 더 잘 도와줄 수 있을 것이다. 번아웃은 심각한 문제이지만, 그것은 좋은 의사소통과 강력한 지지집단을 통해 극복될 수 있다.

stay up late 늦게까지 자지 않고 있다   presentation ⑲발표   barely ⑨거의 ~ 아니게   used to-v (과거에) ~이었다[했었
다]   lately ⑨최근에   depressed ⑱우울한 (depression ⑲우울증)   burnout ⑲번아웃, 극도의 피로 (burn out 에너지
를 다 써버리다)   syndrome ⑲증후군   experience ⑧경험하다   stress out 스트레스를 주다   closely ⑨밀접하게
report ⑧알리다   irregular ⑱불규칙적인   at risk 위험에 처한   employee ⑲직원, 근로자   motivate ⑧동기를 부여하
다   trust ⑧신뢰하다, 믿다   identify ⑧확인하다; *찾다, 발견하다   sign ⑲징후, 징조   condition ⑲상태; *질환
communication ⑲의사소통   support ⑲지지, 도움   [문제] symptom ⑲증상   overcome ⑧극복하다
dissatisfaction ⑲불만족   salary ⑲급여   competition ⑲경쟁   examine ⑧진찰하다, 검사하다   session ⑲기간,
시간

구문 해설

2행   He is **so** tired **that** he can barely keep his eyes open.

- so ~ that ...: 너무 ~하여 …하다

7행   Since the mid-1970s, scientists have been studying about burnout **so that** they **can** *help
workers manage* their stress.

- so that ~ can ...: ~가 …할 수 있도록
- help + 목적어 + (to) 동사원형: ~가 …하도록 돕다

12행   In addition, people with jobs [**that** *require them to work* irregular hours] are also at risk.

- that: 선행사 jobs를 수식하는 주격 관계대명사
- require + 목적어 + to-v: ~가 …하도록 요구하다

Reading 2   p.14

②

해석

학업 스트레스 때문에, 어린 학생들조차 번아웃 증후군을 경험할 수 있다. 하지만, 그것을 예방할 수 있는 방법들이 있다. 첫째로, 중
요도의 순서로 일들을 하는 것이 중요하다. 이것은 당신이 당신의 시간을 잘 관리하도록 도울 것이다. 당신 자신을 위한 시간을 갖는
것 또한 중요하다. 이 시간 동안, 당신은 휴식을 취하거나 운동을 하거나, 심지어 친구를 만날 수도 있다. 이것은 당신의 스트레스 정도
를 줄이고 당신이 다시 공부를 시작할 때 더 생산적이 되도록 도울 것이다. 처음에, 당신은 이 시간 동안 공부를 하지 않는 것에 대해
죄책감을 느낄지도 모른다. 하지만 이러한 자유 시간이 없으면, 당신은 쉽게 에너지를 다 써버릴 수 있다.

어휘

prevent ⑧막다, 예방하다   task ⑲일, 과제   order ⑲순서   importance ⑲중요성   level ⑲정도, 수준   productive
⑱생산하는; *생산적인   guilty ⑱죄책감이 드는

3행　First, **it's** important **to do** tasks in the order of their importance.

• it은 가주어이고, to do는 진주어로 '~하는 것'의 의미

Unit Review
p.15

A Reading 1 hard, irregular, trusted, communication　Reading 2 prevent

B **1** employee **2** order **3** identify **4** closely **5** experience **6** guilty

---

Reading 2 해석

학생들은 중요한 일을 먼저 하고 그들 자신을 위한 자유 시간을 가지면 번아웃 증후군을 예방할 수 있다.

UNIT 03 Origins

Reading 1
pp.16-17

Before Reading　I feel a bit scared, but excited.

1 ①　**2** ④　**3** ①　**4** ③　**5** ③　**6** (1) T (2) F

해석

　　오늘날 대관람차는 놀이공원에서 인기 있는 놀이 기구이다. 그것들은 크고 수직으로 세워진 바퀴이며, 그것들은 가장자리 주변으로 사람들이 타는 객차를 가지고 있다. 바퀴가 돌면서, 승객들은 공원의 멋진 전망을 본다.

　　최초의 대관람차는 1893년에 조지 W.G. 페리스에 의해 발명되었다. 페리스는 엔지니어였고, 그는 일리노이 주의 시카고에서 열린 세계 박람회를 위한 어떤 놀라운 것을 만들어 내기를 원했다. 그는 자신의 발명품이 에펠탑만큼 유명해지기를 바랐다. <u>그리고 다행스럽게도, 그것은 박람회에서 큰 성공을 거두었다.</u>

　　대관람차는 그것의 <u>크기</u> 때문에 특히 인상적이었다. 현대의 대관람차는 보통 20개의 객차가 있고, 각 객차는 오직 소수의 사람들만 수용할 수 있다. 그러나 최초의 관람차는 36개의 커다란 객차들이 있었고, 각 객차에는 60개의 좌석이 있었다. 그래서 2,160명의 사람들이 한 번에 그것을 탈 수 있었다! 그러나 문제는 그것이 운영하기에 너무 비쌌다는 것이었고, 그래서 그것은 1906년까지만 사용되었다. 관람차의 금속은 나중에 재활용되었고, 그것은 제1차 세계 대전 때 USS 일리노이 전함을 짓는 데 사용되었다.

　　<u>비록</u> 최초의 대관람차는 없어졌지만, 그것은 많은 사람들에게 영감을 주었다. 그리고 현재, 여러분은 전 세계의 축제, 박람회, 그리고 놀이공원에서 비슷한 놀이기구를 찾아볼 수 있다.

Ferris wheel 대관람차   ride ⑲ (놀이공원 등에 있는) 놀이 기구 ⑤ 타다   amusement park 놀이공원   upright ⑱ 수직으로 세워 둔   passenger car 객차   edge ⑲ 끝, 가장자리, 모서리   rotate ⑤ 회전하다   invent ⑤ 발명하다 (invention ⑲ 발명)   engineer ⑲ 엔지니어   amazing ⑱ 놀라운   fair ⑲ 박람회   impressive ⑱ 인상적인   original ⑱ 원래의, 최초의   at once 한 번에   operate ⑤ 운영하다   recycle ⑤ 재활용하다   battleship ⑲ 전함   inspire ⑤ 영감을 주다   similar ⑱ 비슷한   carnival ⑲ 카니발, 축제   [문제] beat ⑤ 이기다; *더 낫다, 능가하다   success ⑲ 성공   weight ⑲ 무게   material ⑲ 재료   shut down (공장·가게의) 문을 닫다   cost ⑲ 비용   design ⑤ 설계하다   introduce ⑤ 소개하다

구문 해설

9행   He hoped his invention would be **as famous as** the Eiffel Tower.
  • as + 형용사[부사]의 원급 + as ~: ~만큼 …한[하게]

14행   The problem, however, was **that** it was very expensive *to operate*, so it was only used
  주어   동사   보어(절)
  until 1906.
  • that ~ operate는 be동사 was의 보어절로 '~라는 것'의 의미임
  • to operate: '~하기에'라는 의미로 형용사 expensive를 수식하는 부사적 용법의 to부정사

Reading 2
p.18

③

해석

놀이공원은 수년 동안 그곳의 손님들에게 즐거움을 가져다주었다. 사실, 바켄이라고 불리는 최초의 놀이공원은 1583년 덴마크 코펜하겐에 세워졌다! **(B)** 그 당시, 한 여성이 도시 근처의 숲에서 샘을 발견했다. 코펜하겐의 물은 깨끗하지 않았기 때문에, 많은 사람들이 물을 얻기 위해 그 샘을 방문하기 시작했다. 얼마 지나지 않아, 그곳은 추가적인 사업 기회를 원하고 있었던 연예인들과 판매원들에게 인기 있는 장소가 되었다. **(C)** 그 지역의 명성은 빠르게 높아졌지만, 그곳은 훨씬 후에야 제대로 된 놀이공원이 되었다. 1885년에 건물들과 천막들이 지어졌고, 공원은 전기로 작동되었다. **(A)** 이것은 서커스들과 움직이는 놀이기구들을 그곳으로 끌어들였고, 그곳을 제대로 된 놀이공원으로 만들었다. 요즘, 바켄은 여전히 운영 중이고, 손님들은 대관람차와 82년 된 롤러코스터와 같은 놀이기구를 즐길 수 있다!

어휘

bring ⑤ 가져오다   joy ⑲ 즐거움   found ⑤ 설립하다   attract ⑤ 끌어들이다   proper ⑱ 적절한, 제대로 된   discover ⑤ 발견하다   spring ⑲ 샘   visit ⑤ 방문하다   entertainer ⑲ 연예인   salesman ⑲ 판매원   fame ⑲ 명성   power ⑤ 동력을 공급하다, 작동시키다   electricity ⑲ 전기

1행 In fact, the very first amusement park, [called Bakken], was founded in Copenhagen,

주어 ▲ 동사

Denmark in 1583!

· called Bakken은 the very first amusement park를 수식하는 과거분사구

11행 The area's fame grew quickly, but it did**n't** become a proper amusement park **until** much later.

· not ~ until ...: …한 이후에야 비로소 ~하다

Unit Review

p.19

A Reading 1 invented, famous, expensive, similar Reading 2 spring

B **1** joy **2** found **3** rotate **4** edge **5** discover **6** fame

---

Reading 2 해석

바켄은 샘으로 인기를 얻었고 나중에 세계 최초의 놀이공원이 되었다.

UNIT 04 *Sports*

Reading 1

pp.20-21

Before Reading When I watch soccer games, I can see the referees blow whistles and run alongside players!

1 ① **2** (1) ③ (2) ① (3) ② **3** ② **4** understand the rules of the game **5** ③ **6** ③

해석

잉글랜드 프리미어리그의 프로축구 심판인 마이클 빌이 우리에게 그의 직업에 대해 말한다.

Q 심판은 경기 중에 무엇을 해야 합니까?

A 심판의 주요 임무는 경기를 통제하는 것입니다. 당신은 선수들이 규칙들을 따르도록 확실히 해야 합니다. 그들이 규칙을 어기면 벌칙을 줘야 하고요. 때때로 당신의 결정이 경기 결과를 바꾸기도 하지요.

Q 당신 직업의 장점은 무엇입니까? 혹 단점도 있습니까?

A 가장 큰 장점은 축구 경기를 가까이서 볼 수 있다는 것이지요. 저는 축구를 정말로 좋아하기 때문에 제게는 이것이 재미있습니다. 물론 스트레스 같은 나쁜 점들도 있지요. 선수들, 감독들 그리고 팬들이 당신의 결정에 동의하지 않을 경우 당신에게 소리를 지르고 심지

어는 당신을 공격합니다. 하지만 저는 이 직업에는 나쁜 점들보다는 좋은 점들이 더 많이 있다고 생각합니다.

Q 심판은 어떤 기술을 갖고 있어야 합니까?

A 경기의 규칙들을 이해하고 있어야 합니다. 그렇기 때문에 예전에 선수였던 심판들이 많습니다. 또한 전체 경기 내내 뛰어다니기 때문에 건강해야 합니다. 그리고 마지막으로 예기치 않은 사건들에 대해 신속하게 결정을 내릴 수 있어야 합니다.

Q 어떻게 심판이 됩니까?

A 음, 프로 심판이 되기 위해서는 학교에 다녀야 합니다. 많은 훈련이 필요하죠. 그리고 축구의 경우, 당신이 전국 리그에서 일자리를 얻을 수 있기까지는 10년 이상의 경험이 필요합니다.

어휘

professional *명프로 형전문적인   referee 명(축구·권투 등의) 심판   league 명(스포츠 경기의) 리그, 연맹   make sure 확실하게 하다   break 동깨뜨리다; *(규칙 등을) 어기다   penalty 명벌칙   decision 명결정   yell at ~에게 소리지르다   attack 동공격하다   fit 형건강한   throughout 전~ 내내   whole 형전체의   unexpected 형예기치 않은   national 형국가의; *전국적인   [문제] origin 명기원   relaxed 형편안한   satisfied 형만족한   uninterested 형무관심한   at least 적어도, 최소한

구문 해설

10행   The best thing is (that) I can watch soccer games closely.
　　　　　　　주어　　　　동사　　　　　　　　보어(절)
　　　　　• is 뒤에는 보어절을 이끌어 '~라는 것'이라는 뜻을 나타내는 접속사 that이 생략되어 있음

13행   But I think (that) there are **more** good things about the job **than** bad things.
　　　　　• 비교급 ~ than ...: …보다 더 ~한[하게] (이때의 more는 many의 비교급)

15행   **That's why** there are many referees [who used to be players].

　　　　　• that's why ~: 그것이 ~한 이유이다, 그래서 ~하다 (why는 선행사를 포함하는 관계부사)

Reading 2

⑤

해석

다음은 축구 심판들에 의해 경기 중에 사용되는 몇 가지 도구들이다.

호루라기

심판들은 호루라기의 큰 소리를 이용하여 경기를 통제한다. 짧은 호루라기 소리는 단순한 반칙이 있었음을 나타내는 데 사용된다. 더 길고 큰 호루라기 소리는 심각한 반칙이 있었음을 의미한다. 길고 큰 호루라기 소리는 득점이 있을 때도 사용된다.

시계

시계는 경기의 시간을 재기 위해 사용된다. 대부분의 심판들은 두 개의 시계를 사용한다. 하나는 얼마나 많은 시간이 지났는지를 재고 다른 하나는 부상에 소비된 시간을 잰다.

반칙 카드

옐로카드는 규칙을 어기는 선수들에게 경고하기 위해 사용된다. 레드카드는 선수들에게 그들이 경기에서 퇴장되었음을 알려 주는 데 사용된다.

동전

심판들은 경기 시작 때 동전을 던진다. 이것은 누가 공을 갖고 시작할지와 각 팀이 어느 쪽 골문을 지킬 것인지를 결정한다.

깃발

보조 심판들은 깃발을 가지고 다닌다. 그들은 공이 경기장 밖으로 나갔거나 반칙이 있었음을 나타내기 위해 그것들을 공중으로 들어 올린다.

어휘

tool 똉도구   whistle 똉호루라기   foul 똉반칙, 파울   goal 똉골, 골문   score 뙝득점을 하다   keep track of ~을 놓치지 않고 따라가다   injury 똉부상 (injured 똅부상을 입은)   warn 뙝경고하다   throw out of 퇴장시키다, 쫓아내다   flip 뙝 (손가락으로) 튀기다, 휙 던지다   defend 뙝방어하다   assistant 똉조수 똅*보조의

구문 해설

9행   **One** keeps track of *how much time has passed* and **the other** keeps track of ...

• one ~ the other ...: (둘 중에) 하나는 ~ 다른 하나는 …
• how much time has passed는 keeps track of의 목적어 역할을 하는 간접의문문

Unit Review

p.23

A   Reading 1   controlling, penalty, disagree, rules

B   1 defend   2 assistant   3 referee   4 unexpected   5 national   6 attacked

Reading 1 해석

축구 심판들은 매우 중요한 임무를 가지고 있다. 그들은 경기를 통제하는 것 및 양 팀 모두에게 그것(경기)이 공정하도록 하는 것에 책임이 있다. 만약 어떤 선수가 규칙을 어긴다면 심판은 그 선수에게 벌칙을 주어야 한다. 선수들, 감독들, 그리고 심지어는 관중들과 같은 경기에 관여된 사람들은 종종 심판의 결정에 동의하지 않는다. 성공하기 위해서는, 심판들은 축구의 규칙들에 익숙해야 한다. 그들은 또한 신체적으로 건강해야 하는데 그들은 경기장 위아래로 공을 따라다녀야 하기 때문이다.

UNIT 05 Health

pp.24-25

Before Reading | I think it's rude to burp in public.

1 ② **2** ① **3** showing your appreciation to the cook **4** ③ **5** ① **6** (1) T (2) F

해석

당신은 맛있는 식사를 하고 나서 큰 트림을 해본 적이 있는가? 당신의 부모님은 아마도 당신을 혼내며 "트림하지 말아라! 그것은 실례야."라고 말씀하셨을 것이다. 그러나 트림을 멈추는 것이 가능할까? 그리고 어쨌거나 트림은 정확히 무엇일까?

음, 트림은 당신의 위에서 빠져나오는 공기의 소리이다. 당신의 입에서 빠져나오기 위해서, 그것은 목구멍 뒤에 있는 얇은 근육을 통과해야 한다. 당신의 위에서 빠져나오는 공기가 이 근육을 급하게 지나갈 때… 어어… 그윽! 그것을 멈출 방법은 정말로 없다!

그렇다면 어떻게 공기가 당신의 위 속으로 들어가는 걸까? 자, 모르는 사이에 당신은 보통 매시간 1리터의 공기를 삼킨다. 음식을 먹고 마실 때는 훨씬 더 많이 삼킨다. 따라서 트림은 매우 정상적이다. 사실 몇몇 나라에서는 요리사에게 감사의 뜻을 표하기 위해 음식을 먹은 후에 트림하는 것이 예의이다!

그러나 너무 잦은 트림은 당황스러울 수 있다. 하지만 걱정하지 말아라! 트림을 덜 자주 하는 몇 가지 방법이 있다. 첫째, 입에 음식물을 가득 채운 채로 말하지 말아라. 말하는 동시에 먹는 것은 당신이 더 많은 공기를 삼키게 한다. 둘째, 천천히 먹어라. 빨리 먹는 것은 더 많은 공기가 당신의 위 속으로 들어가게 한다. 셋째, 탄산음료를 마시는 것을 멈춰라. 탄산음료 캔 하나에는 1,800만 개 이상의 공기 방울이 들어 있기 때문에, 캔 하나를 마시는 것은 당신이 몇 시간 동안 트림을 하게 할 수 있다!

어휘

let out ~을 내다[유출하다] burp 몡통트림(을 하다) probably 튀아마 scold 통꾸짖다 rude 혱무례한 exactly 튀정확히 escape 통탈출하다 stomach 몡위 muscle 몡근육 throat 몡목구멍 rush 통돌진하다 swallow 통삼키다 liter 몡리터 normal 혱정상적인 polite 혱예의 바른 appreciation 몡감사 embarrassing 혱당황케 하는 at the same time 동시에 soda 몡탄산음료 bubble 몡거품, 기포 [문제] manner 몡(~s) 예의범절, 예절 (table manner 식사예절) think of A as B A를 B로 여기다

구문 해설

5행   Well, a burp is the sound of air [(which[that] is) escaping from your stomach].

12행   ..., **it** is polite **to burp** after eating *to show* your appreciation to the cook!
- it은 가주어, to burp가 문장의 진주어임
- to show: '~하기 위하여'의 의미로 목적을 나타내는 부사적 용법의 to부정사

16행   Talking and eating at the same time **makes** *you swallow* more air.
            주어   동사   목적어   목적보어
- 주어로 사용된 동명사구는 단수 취급하므로 동사 make는 3인칭 단수형으로 쓰임
- 사역동사(make) + 목적어 + 동사원형: ~가 …하게 하다

④

해석

트림을 하는 것은 인간뿐만이 아니다. 소들도 온종일 목초를 먹기 때문에 자주 트림을 한다. 실제로, 불과 한 마리의 소가 하루에 약 150리터의 메탄가스를 트림을 통해 내뱉는다. 이것은 문제가 되는데, 메탄가스가 지구 온난화를 증가시키기 때문이다. 한 무리의 소가 가정의 자동차 한 대만큼 많은 메탄가스를 만들어 낸다는 것을 안다면 당신은 놀랄 것이다. 그래서 과학자들은 소들의 트림을 줄여 줄 그들을 위한 새로운 먹이에 대해 연구하고 있다. 그들은 클로버와 그 밖의 녹색 잎이 목초보다 소가 트림을 덜 하게 한다는 것을 발견했다. 다행히 소들도 그것들을 먹는 것을 좋아한다!

어휘

methane ⑲메탄   per ⑳~당, ~마다   increase ⑧증가시키다   global warming 지구 온난화   produce ⑧생산하다
cause ⑧일으키다, 야기하다   [문제] diet ⑲식단, 먹이

구문 해설

4행　**It** may surprise you **to know** that ... produces *as much* methane gas *as* a family car.
- It은 가주어, to know 이하가 문장의 진주어임
- as many[much] A as B: B 만큼 많은 A (gas는 셀 수 없는 명사이므로 much를 씀)

Unit Review p.27

| A | Reading 1 | polite, natural, stomach, increases | Reading 2 | global warming |
| B | 1 normal | 2 cause | 3 burp | 4 embarrassing | 5 rude | 6 swallow |

Reading 1 해석

많은 나라에서, 식사 중에 트림하는 것은 예의 바르지 않다. 하지만, 트림하는 것은 지극히 자연스럽다. 그것은 공기가 위에서 갑자기 나갈 때 발생한다. 이 공기는 당황스러운 소리를 내면서 당신의 목의 가는 근육을 급하게 지나간다. 약 1리터의 공기가 매시간 당신의 위로 들어간다. 하지만 당신이 먹으면서 이야기하거나, 빨리 먹거나, 탄산음료를 마시면 이 양은 증가한다. 이러한 것들을 피함으로써, 당신은 트림을 덜 자주 할 수 있을 것이다.

Reading 2 해석

소들로부터 나오는 트림은 지구 온난화를 증가시킬 수 있기 때문에 과학자들은 소들이 트림을 덜 하도록 도울 새로운 먹이를 만들고 있다.

UNIT 06 *Travel*

Reading 1

Before Reading If I had to stay a night in prison, I might feel nervous and scared.

1 ④ **2** ③ **3** ② **4** ③ **5** ② **6** stop them from happening again

해석

나는 여행하는 것을 정말 좋아하지만, 일반적인 관광객은 아니다. 나는 끔찍한 일들이 일어난 유적지를 방문하는 것에 관심이 있다. 그래서 나는 여름방학 동안에 두 곳을 다녀왔다.

첫 번째 장소는 유럽 국가인 라트비아에 있는 카로스타 감옥이었다. 과거에, 그곳은 나치와 러시아인들에 의해 군사 교도소로 사용되었다. 하지만 오늘날 그곳은 호텔이다. 나는 투숙객이었음에도 죄수처럼 대우받았다! 호텔 직원들은 교도관처럼 차려입었고 내가 그들의 말을 듣지 않았을 때 벌을 줬다. 그것은 정말 재미있었지만 약간 무섭기도 했다. 나는 체크아웃을 하고 다시 자유가 되었을 때 정말 안도했다!

나는 또한 남아프리카에 있는 로벤섬 감옥 박물관을 방문했다. 정치범들은 그곳에 수감되곤 했다. 나는 그 섬과 감옥을 견학했다. 내 관광 가이드는 과거에 수감자였다! 그는 내게 자신의 개인적인 경험에 대해 말해주었다. 그는 또한 내게 넬슨 만델라가 18년 동안 살았던 작은 감방을 보여주었다. 그것은 놀라운 여행이었다!

당신은 이러한 장소들을 방문하는 것이 이상하다고 생각할지도 모른다. 하지만 나는 그것이 교육적인 경험이라고 생각한다. 우리는 인류 역사의 암울한 사건들이 다시 일어나는 것을 막기 위해 그것들에 대해 배워야 한다.

어휘

regular ⑱규칙적인; *일반적인   be interested in ~에 관심이 있다   historical site 유적지 (historical ⑱역사적, 역사상의 site ⑲위치, 장소)   terrible ⑱끔찍한   vacation ⑲방학; 휴가   prison ⑲교도소, 감옥 (prisoner ⑲죄수 prison guard 교도관)   military ⑱군사의   guest ⑲손님; *투숙객   treat ⑧대(우)하다, 취급하다   employee ⑲종업원, 고용인 punish ⑧처벌하다, 벌주다   museum ⑲박물관   political ⑱정치적인   former ⑱과거의, 이전의   cell ⑲감방 educational ⑱교육의, 교육적인   [문제] scary ⑱무서운, 겁나는   relieved ⑱안도하는, 다행으로 여기는   rule ⑧통치하다, 지배하다   personal ⑱개인의, 개인적인   extremely ⑨극도로

구문 해설

1행   I'm interested in visiting <u>historical sites</u> [**where** terrible things happened].

16행   You might think **it** is strange **to visit** these places.
   • it은 가주어이고 to visit 이하가 진주어임

17행   We need to learn about dark events in human history **so** (that) we **can** *stop them from happening* again.
   • so (that) ~ can ...: ~가 …할 수 있도록
   • stop + 목적어 + from v-ing: ~가 …하는 것을 막다

④

9/11 그라운드 제로 관광

9/11 추모 기념비

우리는 여러분이 9/11 추모 기념비를 방문하도록 초대합니다. 그것은 쌍둥이 빌딩이 있던 곳인 그라운드 제로에 세워졌습니다. 이곳에서 여러분은 2001년 9월 11일에 일어난 9/11 테러 때 목숨을 잃은 사람들의 이름들을 볼 수 있습니다.

관광 하이라이트

• 그라운드 제로와 9/11 추모 기념비에 대한 90분간의 영어 관광

• 9/11에 직접적인 영향을 받은 뉴욕 시민들이 안내함

• 그날의 사건과 9/11의 영웅들에 대해 더 많이 알 수 있음

관광 방침

• 10분 일찍 도착해 주세요. 늦으면 투어 그룹에 참여할 수 없습니다.

• 가이드에게 여러분의 성함을 말씀해 주세요. 표는 출력하실 필요가 없습니다.

일정 변경 방침

• 관광 일정을 언제든지 위약금 없이 변경할 수 있습니다.

• 관광 일정 변경 후 관광을 하지 않기로 결정할 경우에는 환불되지 않습니다.

memorial ⑲기념비　　attack ⑲공격　　directly ⑨곧장, 직접적으로　　affect ⑧영향을 끼치다　　policy ⑲정책, 방침
reschedule ⑧일정을 변경하다　　refund ⑲환불(금)　　available ⑲구할[이용할] 수 있는　　[문제] on time 시간에 맞추어서

2행　　It was built on Ground Zero, the area [**where** the Twin Towers *used to stand*].

• where: the area를 수식하는 장소를 나타내는 관계부사

• used to-v: ~하곤 했다 (과거의 습관이나 상태를 표현)

4행　　Here, you can read the names of those [**who** lost their lives in the 9/11 attacks], *which*

happened on September 11th, 2001.

• who: 선행사 those를 수식하는 주격 관계대명사

• which: the 9/11 attacks를 선행사로 하는 계속적 용법의 주격 관계대명사

A Reading 1 hotel, prisoners, punish, political, educational

B **1** directly **2** educational **3** refund **4** rescheduled **5** policy **6** personal

Reading 1 해석

나는 비극적인 사건이 일어난 곳들을 방문하는 것을 좋아한다. 라트비아에서는 관광객들이 (이전에) 감옥이었던 호텔에 머물 수 있다. 직원들은 투숙객을 죄수처럼 대우하며, 투숙객이 말을 듣지 않으면 투숙객에게 벌을 주기도 한다. 남아프리카에서는 관광객들이 로벤 섬 감옥 박물관에 방문할 수 있다. 관광 가이드 중 일부는 이전에 정치범이었다. 이 박물관에 방문하는 사람들은 넬슨 만델라의 감방을 볼 수 있다. 이런 종류의 장소를 방문하는 것이 이상하고 무서울 수도 있지만 그것은 매우 교육적이다.

UNIT 07 Teens

Reading 1

pp.32-33

Before Reading When I feel nervous, I try to close my eyes and take a deep breath.

1 ① **2** ③ **3** ④ **4** ③ **5** ② **6** ④

해석

케이 박사님께,

새로운 사람을 만날 때마다 저는 아주 작아진 느낌이 들고 할 말이 전혀 생각나지 않아요. 또 선생님이 수업 시간에 저에게 질문을 하면 굉장히 떨려요. 제 양 볼은 선명한 빨간색으로 변해요. 어떻게 하면 제가 이렇게 부끄러움을 타는 것을 멈출 수 있을까요?

부끄러움을 많이 타는 사람이

우선, 부끄러움을 타는 것은 나쁜 게 아니라는 것을 기억하세요. 많은 사람들이 처음 만나는 사람들과 상황들에 대해 편안함을 느끼게 되는 데에 시간이 약간 필요합니다. 하지만 만일 당신이 정말로 수줍음을 극복하고 싶다면 다음의 유용한 조언들을 따라 보세요.

첫째, 당신이 아는 사람들을 상대로 사소한 대화를 시작하세요. "오늘 뭐 했어?"와 같은 간단한 질문을 해보세요. 그들은 당신의 질문에 대답하는 것을 아주 좋아할 것이고 대화는 쉽게 이어질 것입니다. 둘째, 당신이 말하고 싶은 것을 연습하세요. 몇몇 개의 아이디어를 적어서 그것들을 당신의 방에서 연습해 볼 수도 있습니다. "당신을 만나서 너무 좋습니다." 혹은 "오늘 날씨가 참 좋아요, 그렇죠?"와 같은 몇 가지 것들을 외워 보세요. (대부분의 사람들은 그들이 자유 시간에 즐겨 하는 것을 적어도 한 가지는 갖고 있습니다.) 그러면 당신이 새로운 사람을 만났을 때 당신은 그들과 쉽게 대화할 수 있을 것입니다. 셋째, 당신 자신에게 기회를 주세요! 부끄러움을 타는 많은 사람들은 스스로에게 화가 납니다. 이것은 그들을 더 긴장하게 만들 뿐입니다. 자신을 비난하는 대신, 숨을 깊게 들이쉬고 자신을 격려하세요. 당신은 즉시 기분이 나아질 겁니다! 마지막으로, 당신은 유일하고 특별한 사람이라는 것을 기억하세요. 당신의 수줍음은 그저 당신을 이루는 한 가지 부분일 뿐입니다! 자신만의 스타일을 찾으세요, 왜냐하면 다른 사람들은 당신을 그저 당신이기 때문에 좋아할 테니까요.

케이 박사가

nervous ⑧긴장한, 떨리는   cheek ⑨볼, 뺨   bright ⑧밝은, 선명한   shy ⑧수줍은 (shyness ⑨수줍음)   first of all 우선   comfortable ⑧편안한   situation ⑨상황   overcome ⑧극복하다   continue ⑧계속되다   memorize ⑧암기하다   at least 적어도   blame ⑧비난하다   breath ⑨숨, 호흡   encourage ⑧격려하다   immediately ⑨즉시   unique ⑧독특한, 고유의   [문제] deal with (문제·과제 등을) 처리하다, 해결하다   anger ⑨화, 분노   annoy ⑧짜증나게 하다   greeting ⑨(~s) 인사말   calm down 진정하다   mad ⑧미친; *몹시 화가 난

구문 해설

2행   **Every time** I meet *someone new*, I feel ... and can't think of <u>anything</u> **to say**.
- every time: ((접속사적으로 쓰여)) ~할 때마다 (= whenever)
- someone과 같이 -one으로 끝나는 대명사는 형용사가 그 뒤에서 수식함
- to say는 anything을 수식하는 형용사적 용법의 to부정사

13행   Second, practice **what** you want to say.
- what: 선행사를 포함하는 관계대명사로 '~하는 것'의 의미

21행   Find your own style, because others will like you **for** just being you.
- for: (이유) ~의 이유로

Reading 2   p.34

③

해석

당신이 통학 버스에 올라탈 때 발을 헛디디고 넘어진다. 모두가 웃기 시작하고 당신의 얼굴은 토마토처럼 붉어진다! 걱정하지 마라. 우리는 모두 가끔 얼굴이 붉어진다. 그런데 얼굴이 붉어지는 것은 정확히 무엇일까?

당신이 당황스러울 때 당신의 뇌는 특별한 화학물질을 만든다. 이 화학물질은 당신의 얼굴에 있는 혈관들의 폭을 넓힌다. 보다 많은 혈액이 그것들을 통해 흐르게 되고 당신의 피부는 선명한 붉은색으로 변하게 된다! 연구에 따르면 얼굴이 붉어지는 것은 어른들보다 더 자주 당황하는 십대들 사이에서 가장 흔하다고 한다. 그렇다면 얼굴이 붉어지는 것을 통제하는 것이 가능할까? 그렇지는 않다. 그러나 더 자신감을 가짐으로써 당신은 그것을 유발하는 당혹감을 줄일 수 있다.

어휘

step onto ~에 올라서다   trip ⑧(발이) 걸리다, 헛디디다   blush ⑧얼굴을 붉히다   embarrassed ⑧당황스러운, 당황한 (embarrassment ⑨당혹감)   chemical ⑨화학물질   widen ⑧~의 폭을 넓히다   blood vessel 혈관   flow ⑧흐르다   common ⑧흔한   confident ⑧자신감 있는

8행   Studies show **that** blushing is most common among teenagers, *who* feel ...

　　　• that: show의 목적어절을 이끄는 접속사
　　　• who: teenagers를 선행사로 하는 계속적 용법의 주격 관계대명사

11행   ..., you can reduce the feelings **of** embarrassment [that cause it].

　　　• of: '~이라는'의 뜻으로 동격을 나타냄

Unit Review   p.35

A Reading 1   shy, Start, Write down, angry, be

B **1** confident   **2** encourage   **3** overcome   **4** unique   **5** memorize   **6** blush

UNIT 08 Literature

Reading 1   pp.36-37

Before Reading   I heard that many Jewish people had to move and they were even killed.

1 ②   **2** ④   **3** ②   **4** ②   **5** ④   **6** (1) T   (2) F

해석

안네는 어린 유대인 소녀이다. 나치 독일인들이 그녀의 나라를 점령하자, 그녀는 강제로 숨어있을 수밖에 없다. 그래서 그녀는 일기를 쓰기 시작한다…

1942년 11월 10일 화요일
키티에게

좋은 소식이야! 여덟 번째 사람이 우리와 함께 숨는 데 합류할 거야! 우리는 항상 다른 사람을 위한 방과 음식이 있다고 생각해 왔어. 하지만, 우리는 숨어 있는 것을 도와주는 사람들에게 너무 많은 일을 주는 것에 대해 걱정했어. 하지만 최근, 유대인들에게 일어나고 있는 점점 더 끔찍한 일들에 대한 몇몇 소식들이 있었어. 그래서 아버지는 우리의 보호자들에게 한 사람을 더 숨기는 것에 대해 물어보기로 결정했어. 고맙게도, 그들은 동의했고 "7명과 8명 사이에는 거의 차이가 없어요."라고 말했어. 그래서 우리는 모두 앉아서 늘어나고 있는 우리 식구에 누구를 더할 수 있을지 생각해 보았어. 이것은 어렵지 않았어. 아버지는 자기 친구의 친척들을 모두 거절하셨고, 그래서 우리는 그의 다른 친구의 치과의사를 대신 선택했어. 현재, 그 치과의사는 한 젊은 기독교인 여성과 함께 살고 있지. 우리는 그를 잘 모르지만, 그는 조용하지만 친절한 신사인 것 같아. (모든 신사들은 예의 바르게 행동해야 해.) 우리는 그가 잘 어울릴 것이라고 확신해. 그가 오면 그는 내 방에서 잘 것이기 때문에 우리 언니는 접이식 침대를 사용해야 할 거야. 내 치아 중 하나가 아파왔기 때문에, 우리는

어휘

Jewish 영유대인의 (Jew 명유대인)   take over 탈취[장악]하다   force 동강요하다   hide 동숨다   recently 부최근에   horrible 형끔찍한   protector 명보호자   agree 동동의하다   reject 동거부하다   relative 명친척   dentist 명치과의사   currently 부현재   gentleman 명신사   behave 동처신[행동]하다   politely 부공손히, 예의 바르게   fit in 어울리다, 맞다   tool 명기구, 도구   [문제] take care of ~을 돌보다   lately 부최근에   accept 동받아들이다   up to ~까지

구문 해설

8행   However, we were worried about **giving** too much work to the people [*who* help us hide].
- giving 이하는 전치사 about의 목적어로 쓰인 동명사구
- who: 선행사 the people을 수식하는 주격 관계대명사

12행   So we all sat down **to think** about *who we could add to our growing family.*
- to think: '~하기 위하여'의 의미로 목적을 나타내는 부사적 용법의 to부정사
- who가 이끄는 간접의문문은 동사 think about의 목적어 역할을 함

17행   Because one of my teeth **has been hurting**, we'll *ask him to bring* his dentist tools too!
- has been hurting: '~해오고 있다'라는 의미의 현재완료 진행형
- ask + 목적어 + to-v: ~에게 …해 달라고 부탁하다

Reading 2   p.38

③

해석

'안네 프랑크의 일기'는 한 십대 유대인 소녀의 일기이다. 그것은 제2차 세계 대전 동안 그녀의 가족이 숨어있던 시간에 대해 이야기한다. 전쟁 전에 안네의 가족은 나치 독일인을 피해 네덜란드로 이주했다. 그러나 1940년 독일이 네덜란드를 공격했고, 그 결과 안네의 가족은 다시 한번 위험에 처했다. 숨기 위해서, 그녀의 가족은 암스테르담에서 비밀 장소를 찾았고 1942년 7월 6일에 그곳에서 살기 시작했다. 안네는 이 기간 동안 종종 그녀의 일기에 글을 썼고 그녀의 가족의 경험을 서술했다. (그녀는 매우 조용한 언니와 달리 자신감 넘치고 수다스러운 것으로 알려져 있었다.) 그녀가 마지막으로 일기를 쓴 것은 1944년 8월 1일이었고, 3일 후에 나치 독일 경찰은 그들의 은신처를 찾았다. 그녀가 죽은 지 2년 후인 1947년, 안네의 일기는 전 세계가 그녀의 이야기를 알 수 있도록 출판되었다.

어휘

journal 명일기   be in danger 위험에 처하다   describe 동묘사하다, 기술하다   talkative 형말하기를 좋아하는, 수다스러운   unlike 전~와 달리   death 명죽음   publish 동출판하다

7행   She **was known for** being confident and talkative, unlike her sister [who was very quiet].

         • be known for: ~로 알려지다

8행   The last time [(when) she wrote] was on August 1, 1944, and the Nazi German police
                   주어   동사

     found their hiding place three days later.

         • she 앞에 관계부사 when이 생략되어 있음

Unit Review   p.39

A   **Reading 1**   horrible, father, join, dentist, share   **Reading 2**   hiding

B   **1** journal   **2** talkative   **3** force   **4** horrible   **5** relative   **6** hide

Reading 1 해석

안네는 어린 유대인 소녀였다. 그녀는 여섯 명의 다른 유대인들과 함께 나치 독일인들을 피해 숨어있었다. 그 당시, 끔찍한 일들이 유대인들에게 행해지고 있었다. 그래서 안네의 아버지는 그들의 보호자들에게 한 사람을 더 숨겨달라고 요청했다. 그들의 보호자들이 동의했기 때문에, 같이 숨어 있던 사람들은 누가 그들과 함께 할 것인지 의논했다. 그들은 마침내 치과의사를 불러들이기로 결정했다. 그는 안네와 방을 같이 쓸 것이고, 그들은 그에게 안네의 치아를 확인하기 위해 치과 도구를 가져오라고 할 것이다.

Reading 2 해석

'안네 프랑크의 일기'는 제2차 세계 대전 동안 나치 독일인들로부터 숨어있던 한 유대인 소녀의 경험에 관한 것이다.

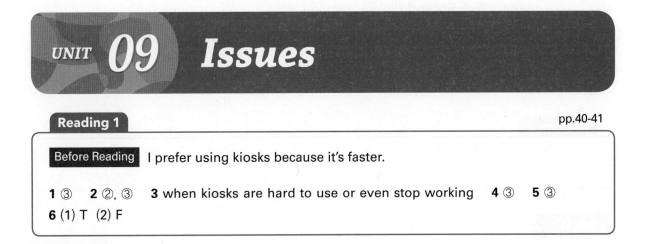

UNIT 09   *Issues*

Reading 1   pp.40-41

Before Reading   I prefer using kiosks because it's faster.

1 ③   **2** ②, ③   **3** when kiosks are hard to use or even stop working   **4** ③   **5** ③
6 (1) T   (2) F

해석

사람들은 종종 기술적인 발전을 좋아하거나 싫어한다. 그럼, 식료품점과 식당에 있는 셀프 서비스 키오스크는 어떤가? 사람들은 키오스크를 사용하여 물건을 선택하거나 스캔한 후 직접 구매한다. 하지만 사람들은 그것들에 대해 어떻게 생각할까?

몇몇 사람들은 셀프 서비스 키오스크 사용을 지지한다. 우선, 키오스크는 사람들이 덜 기다리고 더 빨리 계산하도록 하여, 더 많은 사람들이 그들의 쇼핑을 빨리 끝낼 수 있게 한다. 둘째로, 키오스크는 사람들이 원하는 것을 정확히 선택할 수 있기 때문에 주문의 정확성을 향상시킨다. 심지어 고용주들도 직원들의 임금에 돈을 덜 쓸 수 있기 때문에 이익을 얻는다. 키오스크가 있으면 고객을 돕기 위한 직원들이 거의 필요하지 않다.

반면에, 다른 사람들은 키오스크의 사용을 반대한다. 첫째로, 고객들은 키오스크가 사용하기 힘들거나 심지어 작동을 멈출 때 좌절감을 느낄 수 있다. 그러면 직원들이 와서 문제를 해결해야 한다. 또한, 계산원은 물건을 효율적으로 계산할 수 있는 숙련된 직원이다. 그러므로 계산원 쪽 줄이 빨리 움직인다. 게다가, 키오스크는 고객들이 스캔하는 것과 봉투에 넣는 일을 모두 하게 한다. 아마도 당신은 돈을 받고 쇼핑을 해야 할지도 모른다!

기술은 항상 변화하고 성장하고 있다. 하지만, 그것이 항상 좋은 것만은 아니다. 우리가 사는 방식을 바꾸기 전에 사용자들의 다양한 요구를 고려하는 것이 중요하다.

어휘

hate ⑧싫어하다   technological ⑱기술적인 (technology ⑲기술)   advancement ⑲진보   grocery ⑲식료품   select ⑧선택하다   scan ⑧스캔하다   support ⑧지지하다   check out 계산하다   accuracy ⑲정확성 (accurate ⑱정확한)   order ⑲주문   exactly ⑨정확히   employer ⑲고용주   benefit ⑧이익을 얻다 ⑲혜택, 이득   customer ⑲고객   oppose ⑧반대하다   frustrated ⑱좌절감을 느끼는, 불만스러워 하는   cashier ⑲계산원   skilled ⑱숙련된   efficiently ⑨효율적으로   bag ⑧봉지[가방 등]에 넣다   consider ⑧고려하다   various ⑱다양한   need ⑲(~s) 요구
[문제] communicate ⑧의사소통하다   refuse ⑧거부하다

구문 해설

7행   First of all, kiosks **let people wait** less and **check out** faster, so more people can quickly finish their shopping.

· 사역동사(let) + 목적어 + 동사원형: ~가 …하게 하다

9행   ... kiosks improve the accuracy of orders because people can choose exactly **what** they want.

· what: 선행사를 포함하는 관계대명사로 '~하는 것'의 의미

13행   For one, customers can feel frustrated when kiosks are hard **to use** or even stop working.

· to use: 형용사 hard를 수식하는 부사적 용법의 to부정사로 '~하기에'의 의미

Reading 2

③

해석

어떤 사람들은 인터넷 서비스와 기술에 쉽게 접근하고 그것들을 사용할 수 있는 능력을 가지고 있는 반면, 다른 사람들은 그렇지 않다. 이 차이를 정보 격차라고 한다. 이 용어는 기술을 사용할 수 있는 재정적, 기술적 능력을 모두 포함한다. 이러한 격차는 교육받은 사람과 교육받지 못한 사람 사이뿐만 아니라 선진국과 개발도상국 사이에도 존재한다. 일반적으로 기술에 익숙한 사람들에게 더 많은 기회가 주어진다. 반면에 (기술에) 접근이 한정된 사람들은 다른 사람들과 의사소통할 방법이 더 적고 직업 선택지도 더 적다. 또한, 온라

인 교육의 증가로, 인터넷 자원이 부족한 사람들은 종종 그들의 능력을 발전시키지 못한다. 분명히, 기술은 세상의 더 중요한 부분이 되었다. 그러므로, 이 문제를 해결하기 위해서는 개선된 정부 정책들과 교육 프로그램들이 필요할 것이다.

어휘

ability 명 능력   gap 명 차이   digital divide 정보 격차   term 명 용어   include 동 포함하다   financial 형 금융[재정]의 technical 형 기술적인   exist 동 존재하다   developed country 선진국   underdeveloped country 개발도상국 educated 형 교육 받은   uneducated 형 교육 받지 못한   available 형 이용 가능한   limited 형 제한된, 한정된   access 명 접근   option 명 선택권   increase 명 증가   education 명 교육   lack 동 ~이 없다, 부족하다   resource 명 자원 develop 동 개발시키다   obviously 부 분명히   issue 명 문제   [문제] knowledge 명 지식

구문 해설

2행   The term includes **both** the financial **and** technical ability [*to use* technology].

• both A and B: A와 B 둘 다
• to use: both the financial and technical ability를 수식하는 형용사적 용법의 to부정사로 '~하는'의 의미

3행   This divide exists between developed and underdeveloped countries **as well as** between *the educated* and *the uneducated*.

• B as well as A: A뿐만 아니라 B도 (= not only A but also B)
• the + 형용사: ~한 사람들

5행   Generally, more chances are available to those [**who** *are used to* technology].

• who: those를 수식하는 주격 관계대명사
• be used to + 명사: ~에 익숙하다

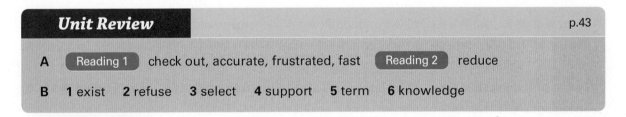

Unit Review   p.43

A   Reading 1   check out, accurate, frustrated, fast   Reading 2   reduce

B   **1** exist   **2** refuse   **3** select   **4** support   **5** term   **6** knowledge

Reading 2 해석

정보 격차, 즉 쉽게 인터넷에 접근할 수 있는 사람들과 그렇지 못한 사람들 사이의 차이를 줄이기 위해 정부 정책들과 교육 프로그램들이 필요하다.

UNIT 10 Jobs

Reading 1

pp.44-45

Before Reading They usually search for people in need and provide them with important services for free.

1 ④ **2** ③ **3** ④ **4** ④ **5** ② **6** ③

해석

나는 안과 의사이지만 대부분의 안과 의사들처럼 진료소나 일반 병원에서 일하지 않는다. 사실 내가 일하는 병원은 세상에 딱 한 종류밖에 없는 것이다. 그것은 '날아다니는 안과 병원'으로, 비행기 안에 있는 병원이다! 1982년부터 이 비행기 병원은 비영리 기구인 오르비스에 의해 운영되어 왔다.

왜 오르비스 안과 병원이 비행기 안에 있어야 할까? 많은 가난한 국가들은 최상의 안과 치료를 제공할 적절한 장비나 시설을 갖고 있지 않다. 어떤 지역에는 병원이 아예 없다! 그래서 우리는 가는 곳마다 우리에게 필요한 모든 장비를 갖고 가야 한다.

우리는 방글라데시, 에티오피아, 인도 같은 여러 나라들에 있는 수백만 명의 사람들을 치료해 왔다. 그렇게 많은 사람들을 도울 수 있는 것은 우리의 일을 정말 가치 있게 만든다. 나처럼 오르비스에서 일하는 다른 모든 사람들은 자원봉사자들이다. 이는 간호사들부터 조종사들까지 모든 사람들을 포함한다.

무료로 의학적 치료를 제공하는 것 외에, 오르비스 의사들은 날아다니는 병원 안에서 현지 의사들에게 훈련을 제공한다. 이것은 중요하다. 이는 우리가 한 나라를 떠난 후에도 사람들이 여전히 그들의 현지 의사들로부터 안과 치료를 받을 수 있게 됨을 의미한다.

어휘

normal ⑧보통의 **run** ⑧달리다; *운영하다 **nonprofit** ⑧비영리의 **organization** ⑲단체, 기구 **equipment** ⑲장비 **facility** ⑲(~ies) 시설 **care** ⑲걱정; *치료 **area** ⑲지역 **treat** ⑧대하다; *치료하다 **million** ⑲100만 **worthwhile** ⑧가치 있는 **volunteer** ⑲자원봉사자 ⑧자원하다 **free** ⑧자유로운; *무료의 **medical** ⑧의학적인 **local** ⑧현지의, 그 지역의 [문제] **disease** ⑲질병 **short-term** ⑧단기간의 (↔ **long-term** ⑧장기간의) **challenging** ⑧도전적인 **meaningful** ⑧의미 있는, 중요한

구문 해설

3행 It's the "Flying Eye Hospital," a hospital on an airplane!

10행 So we have to bring all the equipment [(that) we need] with us **wherever** we go.

· equipment 뒤에는 목적격 관계대명사 that이 생략되어 있음
· wherever: ~하는 어디든지

13행 Being able to help so many people really ***makes*** our work worthwhile.
주어 / 동사 / 목적어 / 목적보어

· makes: 주어로 사용된 동명사구는 단수 취급하므로 동사 make는 3인칭 단수형으로 쓰임

- 사역동사(make) + 목적어 + 형용사: ~을 …하게 만들다

Reading 2   p.46

④

해석

당신은 아마도 적십자에 대해 들어봤을 것이다. 그린피스와 국제앰네스티, 그리고 국경 없는 의사회는 어떤가? **(C)** 이들은 모두 잘 알려진 NGO들이다. NGO는 비정부단체를 의미한다. 이 단체들은 정부들이 할 수 없는 방법으로 사람들을 돕는다. **(A)** 예를 들어, 세계 어디든지 재난이 있으면 적십자와 국경 없는 의사회는 그곳에 가서 목숨을 구할 수 있다. **(B)** 비슷한 방법으로, 그린피스는 환경을 보호하기 위해 일하고 국제앰네스티는 인권을 보호한다. 전 세계에는 수백만 개의 더 작은 NGO들도 있다. 이들 거의 모두가 자원봉사자들을 필요로 한다. 그러니 그중 하나에 자원해 보는 게 어떤가?

어휘

amnesty 명사면   border 명국경   disaster 명재난   similar 형비슷한   environment 명환경   protect 동보호하다   human right 인권   well-known 형유명한, 잘 알려진   stand for ~을 의미하다   non-governmental 형비정부의

구문 해설

10행   These organizations help people in ways [governments are unable to (help)].

- 선행사 the way[ways]와 관계부사(how)는 함께 쓰일 수 없고, 둘 중 하나가 생략되어야 함
- governments are unable to 뒤에는 같은 동사의 반복을 피하기 위해 help가 생략됨

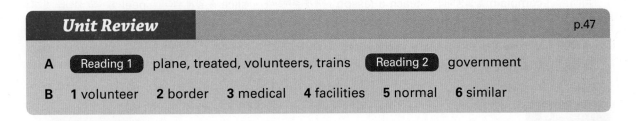

Unit Review   p.47

A Reading 1   plane, treated, volunteers, trains   Reading 2   government

B **1** volunteer   **2** border   **3** medical   **4** facilities   **5** normal   **6** similar

Reading 1 해석

오르비스는 비행기에 있는 병원을 운영하는 비영리 기구이다. '날아다니는 안과 병원'으로 알려진 그 단체는 사람들이 안과 치료를 받을 수 없는 전 세계의 가난한 국가들로 이동한다. 그리고 이 놀라운 병원은 이미 수백만 명의 사람들을 치료해왔다. 게다가 오르비스에서 일하는 모든 사람들은 조종사들을 포함하여, 자원봉사자들이다. 오르비스는 또한 날아다니는 안과 병원이 떠난 후에 환자들이 여전히 좋은 치료를 받을 수 있도록 그 단체가 방문하는 나라의 현지 의사들을 훈련한다.

Reading 2 해석

비정부단체들은 정부가 할 수 없는 방식으로 사람들과 환경을 돕지만, 그들은 그들을 도와줄 자원봉사자들이 필요하다.

UNIT 11 Food

Reading 1

pp.48-49

Before Reading I don't know exactly, but I guess maybe a snack company made them.

1 ④ **2** ④ **3** ③ **4** ② **5** ② **6** (1) F (2) T

해석

당신의 동네에 있는 어떤 식품점에 가더라도 당신은 색색의 많은 감자칩 봉지를 볼 것이다. 다양한 맛과 모양과 크기로 구할 수 있는 감자칩은 스낵을 좋아하는 사람들에게 인기 있는 선택지이다.

그것들은 1853년에 뉴욕 근교의 한 식당에서 조지 크럼이라는 요리사에 의해 발명되었다. 그 당시에 미국에서는 두껍게 자른 감자튀김이 인기 있었다. 그러나 어느 날 한 까다로운 손님이 그의 감자튀김이 너무 두껍다고 계속 불평을 했다. 그래서 크럼은 그에게 주의를 주기로 결심했다. 그는 몇 개의 감자를 포크를 가지고 먹을 수 없을 정도로 얇게 썰어서 그 손님에게 내놓았다. 놀랍게도, 그 손님은 그것을 아주 좋아했다! 다른 손님들도 그 새로운 스낵을 먹어보고 싶어 했고, 크럼은 그것을 메뉴에 추가했다.

감자칩은 곧 미국 북동부 전역에서 인기를 얻게 되었다. 하지만 그것들은 만들거나 저장하기가 쉽지 않았다. 그것들은 손으로 껍질을 벗기고 얇게 썬 뒤 나무 통에 보관해야만 했다. 그러나 감자칩을 대량 생산할 수 있는 기계가 곧 발명되었고, 그것을 오랫동안 신선하게 보관할 수 있는 왁스를 바른 봉지가 개발되었다.

아마도 다음번에 당신이 가게에서 감자칩 한 봉지를 살 때 당신은 그것이 어떻게 그토록 인기 있는 스낵이 되었는지에 대한 이야기를 기억하게 될 것이다.

어휘

neighborhood ⑨동네, 이웃   flavor ⑨맛, 풍미   shape ⑨모양   choice ⑨선택, 선택지   troublesome ⑧성가신, 골치 아픈   complain ⑧불평하다   teach a lesson ~에게 훈계하다   slice ⑧얇게 썰다   peel ⑧~의 껍질을 벗기다   store ⑧저장하다   wooden ⑧나무로 된   barrel ⑨(목재·금속으로 된) 통   machine ⑨기계   mass-produce ⑧대량 생산하다   wax-coated ⑧왁스를 바른   [문제] serve ⑧(음식을) 제공하다, 차려내다   regret ⑨후회   disappointment ⑨실망   by chance 우연히   taste ⑧~의 맛이 나다

구문 해설

1행   **Go into** any food store in your neighborhood, **and** you will see ...
- 명령문 + and ~: …해라, 그러면 ~할 것이다

10행   He ┌ sliced some potatoes **so** *thin* **that** they couldn't be eaten with a fork
        │ and
        └ gave them to the customer.
- so ~ that ...: …할 정도로 ~한[하게]
- thin은 형용사로도 쓰이고 부사로도 쓰이나 여기서는 부사로 쓰임

24

16행 However,

```
┌ machines were soon invented [that could mass-produce potato chips],
│
and
│
└ wax-coated bags were developed [that could keep them fresh …].
```

· 2개의 that은 각각 machines와 wax-coated bags를 수식하는 주격 관계대명사

Reading 2   p.50

①

해석

수백 년 동안 감자는 영국과 북미에서 가장 흔한 식품이었다. 그러므로 많은 영어 관용구가 'potato(감자)'라는 단어를 포함하고 있는 것은 놀랄 일이 아니다. 예를 들어, 어떤 것의 'meat and potatoes(고기와 감자)'는 그것의 가장 중요한 부분을 의미한다. 반면에 'small potatoes(작은 감자)'는 중요하지 않은 것을 의미한다. 'hot potato(뜨거운 감자)'는 아무도 그것에 대해 얘기하고 싶어 하지 않는 성가신 주제이다. 그리고 당신은 'couch potato(소파 감자)'라는 말을 들어보았는가? 그것은 하루 종일 앉아서 TV 보는 것을 좋아하는 사람이다. 그렇다면 'mouse potato(마우스 감자)'는 무엇인지 짐작할 수 있겠는가? 그렇다! 그것은 하루 종일 컴퓨터를 사용하는 것을 좋아하는 사람이다!

어휘

thus ⑨그러므로, 따라서   meat ⑲고기   couch ⑲소파   [문제] idiom ⑲관용구   contain ⑧포함하다   origin ⑲기원
traditional ⑲전통적인   recipe ⑲조리법   dish ⑲접시; *요리   joke ⑲농담

구문 해설

2행 Thus **it's not surprising that** many English idioms contain the word "potato."
· it's not surprising (that) ~: ~은 놀랄 일이 아니다 (it은 가주어, that절은 진주어)

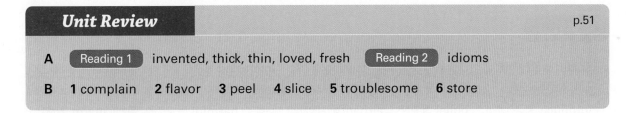

A Reading 1 invented, thick, thin, loved, fresh   Reading 2 idioms
B **1** complain   **2** flavor   **3** peel   **4** slice   **5** troublesome   **6** store

Reading 1 해석

감자칩은 인기 있는 간식이다. 조지 크럼이라는 이름의 한 남자가 1853년에 그것을 발명했다. 그는 그의 식당에서 자주 감자튀김을 만드는 요리사였다. 어느 날, 한 손님이 그의 감자튀김이 너무 두껍다고 불평을 했다. 짜증이 나서, 크럼은 감자 몇 개를 최대한 얇게 썰어서 그의 손님에게 주었다. 놀랍게도, 그 손님은 그것을 정말 좋아했다. 곧, 그것은 매우 유명해졌다. 감자칩을 대량 생산하기 위해 기계가 발명되었고, 감자칩은 신선하게 유지하기 위해 왁스를 바른 봉지에 보관되었다.

감자는 영국과 북미에서 오랫동안 가장 흔한 음식이었기 때문에, 많은 영어 관용구가 'potato(감자)'라는 단어를 포함한다.

UNIT 12 Science

Reading 1
pp.52-53

Before Reading I have seen a spider coming down from its web, but not making webs.

1 ④ **2** ② **3** ③ **4** ② **5** ④ **6** like to spend time alone

해석

거미줄은 당신의 침대 아래, 당신의 옷장 안, 그리고 천장 위 등 어디에나 있다. 당신은 그것이 전혀 특별하지 않다고 생각할지도 모른다. (인간을 아프게 할 수 있는 거미는 불과 몇 종류밖에 없다.) 그러나 과학자들은 거미들이 거미줄을 만들기 위해 사용하는 물질인 거미줄 실에 대해 더 알게 되는 데에 매우 관심이 있다. 그것은 몹시 튼튼하기 때문에 사람들의 흥미를 끈다. 당신은 그것을 구부리거나 늘일 수는 있지만, 그것을 끊기는 힘들다. 어떤 점에 있어서는 거미줄 실이 강철보다 더 튼튼하다!

과학자들은 제품을 만들기 위해 거미줄 실을 이용하는 방법을 연구하고 있다. 그들은 그것이 경찰이나 군인을 돕는 데 사용될 수 있을 것이라고 생각한다. 거미줄 실로 만들어진 옷은 총탄으로부터 그들을 보호할 것이다. 그것은 또한 더 좋은 자동차 에어백을 만드는 데도 사용될 수 있다. 거미줄 실로 만들어진 에어백은 더 부드럽고 승객에게도 덜 위험할 것이다. 그리고 마지막으로, 의사들은 거미줄 실을 사용하여 깊게 베인 상처를 치료할 수 있기를 바란다. 거미줄 실은 이 베인 상처들이 봉해지는 것을 도울 수 있으므로, 그것(상처)들은 더 빨리 나을 수 있다.

그러나 한 가지 문제가 있다. 거미들로부터 실을 모으는 것이 어렵다는 것이다. 그들은 혼자서 시간을 보내는 것을 좋아하므로 '거미 농장'을 만드는 것은 불가능하다. 대신에 과학자들은 거미줄 실을 만드는 비밀을 발견하기 위해 노력하고 있다. 만일 그들이 그것을 만드는 법을 알 수 있다면, 더 많은 유용한 제품들을 만드는 것이 가능할 것이다.

어휘

spider web 거미줄(집)   closet 몡옷장, 벽장   ceiling 몡천장   interested 혱관심 있어 하는 (interest 통흥미를 끌다)
silk 몡명주실, 비단   material 몡물질   bend 통구부리다   stretch 통늘이다   steel 몡강철   product 몡제품
(produce 통생산하다)   bullet 몡총탄   airbag 몡(자동차의) 에어백   harmful 혱해로운; *위험한 (harm 통해치다)
passenger 몡승객   cut 몡베인 상처   heal 통(상처·병 등을) 고치다; *낫다   collect 통모으다   [문제] strength 몡힘
emphasize 통강조하다   injury 몡부상

구문 해설

4행   ... learning more about <u>spider silk</u>, <u>the material</u> [(that) they use **to make** their webs].

• they use 앞에는 목적격 관계대명사 that 또는 which가 생략됨

26

• to make: '〜하기 위하여'의 의미로 목적을 나타내는 부사적 용법의 to부정사

9행   Scientists are studying **how to use** the silk to make products.

• how to-v: 〜하는 방법

11행   Clothes [(that are) made from spider silk] would protect them from bullets.

• made 앞에 '주격 관계대명사 + be동사'가 생략되어 있음

Reading 2   p.54

②

해석

많은 사람들은 거미를 싫어한다. 그들은 모든 거미들이 위험하다고 생각해서, 다시 생각하지 않고 그것들을 죽인다. **(B)** 그러나 사실 사람들을 다치게 할 수 있는 거미는 불과 몇 종류밖에 없다. 대부분의 거미는 사실 우리에게 도움이 된다. **(A)** 이것은 거미들이 곤충들을 먹기 때문인데, 그중에는 사람들에게 해로울 수 있는 것들도 포함되어 있다. 또한 그것들이 곤충을 죽이기 위해 사용하는 독인 거미 독은 언젠가 농부들이 농작물을 보호하는 데 이용될 수 있다. **(C)** 이는 정말로 유용한데, 거미독은 천연이어서 위험한 살충제보다 인간에게 더 안전하기 때문이다. 그러므로 당신이 거미에 대해 듣는 모든 것을 믿지는 마라. 다음에 당신이 거미를 보게 되면 그것을 괴롭히지 마라. 그냥 내버려 둬라.

어휘

dislike ⑧싫어하다   second thought 재고(다시 생각함)   insect ⑨곤충   including ⑳〜을 포함하여   venom ⑨(독사 등의) 독액   poison ⑨독, 독물   crop ⑨(농)작물   hurt ⑧다치게 하다, 아픔을 주다   natural ⑱천연의   bother ⑧괴롭히다

구문 해설

3행   This is because spiders eat insects, including **ones** [that can be harmful to people].

• ones: insects를 가리키는 대명사

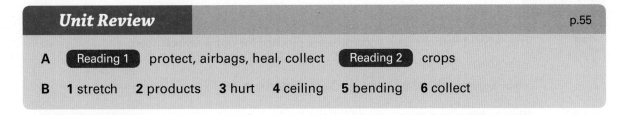

Unit Review   p.55

A   Reading 1   protect, airbags, heal, collect   Reading 2   crops
B   **1** stretch   **2** products   **3** hurt   **4** ceiling   **5** bending   **6** collect

Reading 2 해석

많은 사람들이 거미를 싫어하기는 하지만, 거미는 우리에게 도움이 되고 그들의 독은 미래에 <u>농작물</u>을 보호하는 데 유용할지도 모른다.

Reading 1

Before Reading I might think a festival or advertising campaign is going on.

1 ②   **2** ③   **3** Saint Patrick used the three-leaf clover to teach about Christianity   **4** ③
5 ③   **6** ①

해석

오늘은 3월 17일이고, 당신은 소란스러운 퍼레이드의 한가운데에 서 있다. 사람들은 춤을 추며 지나가고 당신이 보는 곳마다 클로버가 있다. 그러다 갑자기 누군가가 당신을 꼬집는다! 그들은 왜 그렇게 할까? 자, 주변을 둘러보라. 모든 사람들과 모든 것이 녹색이다. 와, 심지어 강조차 녹색 물이 흐르고 있고, 당신을 꼬집은 소녀는 녹색 주스를 마시고 있다! 아니, 이것은 꿈이 아니다. 이날은 성 패트릭 기념일이고, 당신은 녹색 옷을 입지 않아서 꼬집혔다.

성 패트릭 기념일은 노래, 퍼레이드, 녹색 음료와 녹색 음식에만 관한 것이 아니다. 이날은 4세기에 영국에 살았던 한 성인을 기념하는 날이다. 성 패트릭은 불과 16세 때 아일랜드에 노예로 보내졌고, 탈출했지만 몇 년 후에 성직자가 되어 돌아왔다. 그는 여생을 기독교를 전파하며 보냈다. 하지만 왜 온통 녹색이냐고 묻고 싶은가? 음, 전설에 의하면 그가 세 잎 클로버를 이용하여 기독교에 대해 가르쳤다고 한다.

그러니 서둘러 무언가 녹색인 것을 입어라. 그러면 당신 주변의 누군가가 당신에게 키스할지도 모른다. 왜일까? (네 잎 클로버는 행운의 상징이다.) 성 패트릭 기념일에 녹색 옷을 입고 있는 사람에게 키스하면 행운이 오기 때문이다!

어휘

noisy ⑱소란스러운   parade ⑲퍼레이드, 행진   clover ⑲클로버, 토끼풀   suddenly ⑭갑자기   pinch ⑧꼬집다   celebrate ⑧축하하다, 기념하다   holy ⑱성스러운   slave ⑲노예   Ireland ⑲아일랜드 (Irish ⑱아일랜드의)   escape ⑧탈출하다   priest ⑲성직자   rest ⑲*나머지; 휴식   spread ⑧퍼뜨리다, 전파하다   Christianity ⑲기독교   legend ⑲전설   symbol ⑲상징   [문제] costume ⑲복장   competition ⑲경쟁; *시합   environmental ⑱환경의   in memory of ~의 기념으로   touching ⑱감동적인

구문 해설

7행   This is Saint Patrick's Day, and you were pinched **for** *not wearing* green.

• for: (이유) ~의 이유로

• not wearing: 동명사의 부정은 앞에 not 또는 never를 써서 표현함

11행   (Being) **Taken** as a slave ... just 16, Saint Patrick escaped, *yet* returned years later as a priest.

• Taken ... just 16은 앞에 Being이 생략된 분사구문으로, 수동형 분사구문에서 being은 주로 생략함

(← Though he was taken as a slave ... just 16)

• yet: '그럼에도 불구하고', '하지만'이라는 의미의 접속사

13행　Well, legend **has it that** he used the three-leaf clover to teach about Christianity.

　　　　• have it that ~: ~라고 말하다[표현하다]

Reading 2　　　　　　　　　　　　　　　　　　　　　　　　　　　　　　　　　p.58

②

해석

재미있는 녹색 파티에 오세요!

O'Reilly 가족이 성 패트릭 기념일 파티에 당신을 초대합니다!
파티는 다음 주 토요일인 3월 14일 오후 7시에 시작합니다.
당신은 아일랜드 전통 음식과 음악, 춤을 즐길 수 있습니다.
맛있는 녹색 탄산음료와 녹색 쿠키, 녹색 사탕이 있을 겁니다!
파티는 뒤뜰에서 4시간 동안 계속될 겁니다.
친구들이나 가족들을 데려오셔도 됩니다.
몇몇 분의 행운의 손님들께는 깜짝 선물이 있을 겁니다.
자신의 컵 바닥에 그려진 네 잎 클로버를 발견하는 분은 누구든지 멋진 선물을 받게 됩니다!
아무것도 가져오실 필요 없습니다.
그냥 녹색 옷만 꼭 입으세요!
파티에서 뵙겠습니다!

어휘

yummy 형 맛있는　　go on 계속되다　　surprise 명 뜻밖의 선물　　guest 명 초대손님　　bottom 명 밑바닥　　[문제] host 동 주최하다, 진행하다

구문 해설

8행　**Anyone who** finds a four-leaf clover [(that is) drawn … cup] will *be given* a nice gift!

　　　　• anyone who: ~하는 사람은 누구든지
　　　　• A is given B: A에게 B가 주어지다 ('A에게 B를 주다'라는 뜻의 'give A B'의 수동태임)

Unit Review　　　　　　　　　　　　　　　　　　　　　　　　　　　　　　p.59

A　Reading 1　pinch, holy, slave, spreading

B　**1** spread　**2** escape　**3** bottom　**4** surprise　**5** holy　**6** noisy

Reading 1   pp.60-61

Before Reading   A QR code is a square image with multiple boxes and dots. It can be scanned by the camera on a mobile phone.

1 ④   **2** ②   **3** the three large squares in the corners of the code   **4** ②   **5** ③   **6** ②

해석

일반적으로 QR 코드라고 불리는 퀵 리스폰스(quick response) 코드는 정보를 저장하고 공유하는 인기 있는 방법이 되고 있다. 그것들은 바코드와 비슷하다. (오늘날, 대부분의 QR 코드는 스마트폰으로 스캔된다.) 하지만 선을 사용하는 대신, 그것들은 정사각형들과 검은 점들을 사용한다. 여러분은 그것들을 제품과 광고를 포함한 많은 곳에서 찾을 수 있다. 그런데 그것들은 어떻게 작동할까?

먼저, QR 판독기는 코드의 모서리에 있는 세 개의 큰 정사각형들로 QR 코드를 식별한다. 그리고 나서 판독기는 코드를 더 작은 부분들로 나누고 그것들을 검사한다. 각 부분의 패턴을 인식하기 위해, 판독기는 그것이 반사하는 빛의 양을 측정한다. 이것은 검은색은 빛을 흡수하지만, 흰색은 빛을 반사하기 때문에 가능하다. 패턴들이 인식되면, 코드에 저장된 정보에 접근할 수 있다.

QR 코드는 놀랍도록 유용하다. 그것들은 사용하기 편리하고 많은 양의 정보에 쉽게 접근할 수 있게 한다. 게다가, 그것들은 공간을 절약하는 훌륭한 해결책이다. 예를 들어, 기업들은 제품의 세부 정보와 사용 설명서를 고객들에게 제공하기 위해 QR 코드를 사용할 수 있다. 이렇게 하면, 그들은 제품의 포장에 그것들을 인쇄할 필요가 없다. 이렇게 많은 용도를 가지고 있으므로, QR 코드가 왜 이제 거의 모든 산업에서 사용되는지 쉽게 알 수 있다.

어휘

response ⑲응답   typically ⑨일반적으로   share ⑧공유하다   be similar to ~와 비슷하다   barcode ⑲바코드
scan ⑧스캔하다   dot ⑲점   advertisement ⑲광고   reader ⑲판독기   identify ⑧인식하다   section ⑲부분
examine ⑧검사하다   recognize ⑧인식하다   measure ⑧측정하다   reflect ⑧반사하다   absorb ⑧흡수하다
access ⑧접근하다 ⑲접근   incredibly ⑨믿을 수 없을 정도로, 엄청나게   convenient ⑱편리한   solution ⑲해결책
detail ⑲세부 정보   instruction manual 사용 설명서   package ⑲포장   industry ⑲산업   [문제] rival ⑲경쟁자
effective ⑱효과적인   be composed of ~로 구성되다   function ⑧기능하다

구문 해설

1행   <u>Quick response codes</u>, **typically called QR codes**, <u>are becoming</u> <u>a popular way</u> [*to store*
         주어   동사

and (*to*) *share* information].
- typically called QR codes는 Quick response codes를 보충 설명하는 과거분사구
- to store and (to) share: a popular way를 수식하는 형용사적 용법의 to부정사로 '~하는'의 의미

11행   **In order to recognize** the pattern in each section, the reader measures <u>the amount of
         light</u> [(which[that]) it reflects].

- in order to-v: ~하기 위하여
- it 앞에 목적격 관계대명사 which[that]가 생략되어 있음

13행 **Once** the patterns are recognized, <u>the information</u> [stored in the code] <u>can be accessed</u>.

                                            주어 ▲   동사

- once: '(일단) ~하면'이라는 의미의 부사절을 이끄는 접속사
- stored in the code: the information을 수식하는 과거분사구

Reading 2   p.62

⑤

해석

  1994년, 일본의 자동차 부품 회사인 덴소 웨이브가 최초의 QR 코드를 발명했다. 그들은 생산 중에 그들의 부품을 추적할 수 있는 더 나은 방법을 원했다. 바코드는 이 목적을 위해서는 너무 제한적이었다. 그것들은 위에서 아래로 스캔될 수만 있기 때문에 많은 정보를 담을 수 없다. 하지만 QR 코드는 위에서 아래로 그리고 오른쪽에서 왼쪽으로 스캔될 수 있다. 이것은 그것들이 훨씬 더 많은 양의 정보를 저장할 수 있다는 것을 의미한다. 실제로, 그것들은 텍스트를 4,000자까지 담을 수 있다. 덴소 웨이브가 QR 시스템을 만들었기 때문에, 그들은 그것에 대한 소유권을 가지고 있다. 하지만, 그 회사는 이러한 소유권을 사용하지 않기로 결정했다. 이것은 누구나 QR 코드를 자유롭게 사용할 수 있다는 것을 의미한다.

어휘

part 똉일부; *부품 keep track of ~을 기록하다; *추적하다 production 똉생산 limiting 똉제한하는 purpose 똉목적 up to ~까지 create 똉창조[창작]하다 own 똉소유하다 right 똉권리, (~s) 소유권(지적 재산권) decide 똉결정하다 freely 똉자유롭게 [문제] replace A with B A를 B로 대체하다

구문 해설

7행 **Since** Denso Wave created the QR system, they own the rights to it.
- since: '~하기 때문에'라는 의미의 부사절을 이끄는 접속사

8행 However, the company decided **not to use** these rights.
- not to use: to부정사의 부정은 to 앞에 not 또는 never를 써서 표현함

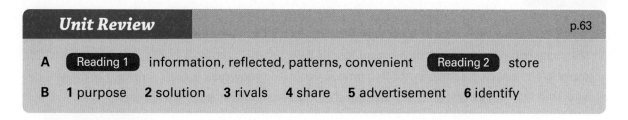

Unit Review   p.63

A   `Reading 1` information, reflected, patterns, convenient `Reading 2` store

B   **1** purpose **2** solution **3** rivals **4** share **5** advertisement **6** identify

Reading 1 해석

QR 코드 또는 퀵 리스폰스(quick response) 코드는 정사각형들과 검은색 점들에 정보를 저장하고 공유한다. QR 판독기는 반사되

고 있는 빛의 양을 측정하여 코드의 각 부분을 주의 깊게 검사한다. 이것은 판독기가 코드의 패턴들을 인식하고 저장된 정보에 접근할 수 있게 한다. 요즘, QR 코드는 이렇게 편리한 방식으로 많은 데이터를 저장할 수 있기 때문에 매우 인기가 있다.

Reading 2 해석

덴소 웨이브는 더 많은 정보를 저장하는 방법으로 QR 코드를 발명했고, 그 회사는 누구나 이 기술을 자유롭게 사용할 수 있도록 했다.

UNIT 15 The Arts

Reading 1
pp.64-65

Before Reading Yes, I love the beautiful sound of string instruments!

1 ② **2** ② **3** ③ **4** ④ **5** play Paganini's famous violin for one day **6** ②

해석

수백만 달러의 가치가 있는 악기가 있다고 말한다면 당신은 믿겠는가? 그것은 사실이다. 그 악기는 '캐논'이라고 불리는 바이올린이다. 그것은 1743년에 가장 유명한 바이올린 제작자들 중 한 명인 Giuseppe Guarneri에 의해 만들어졌다.

캐논은 매우 재능 있는 이탈리아의 바이올리니스트인 Niccolò Paganini에 의해 이름이 붙여졌다. 그는 그것의 소리가 아주 강력했기 때문에 그것을 이렇게 불렀다. 1802년에 그 악기를 선물로 받은 후, 그는 다른 바이올린으로 연주하는 것을 즐기지 않았다. Paganini는 캐논을 그 어떤 것보다 더 좋아했다.

Paganini가 1840년에 사망했을 때, 그 바이올린은 관리될 수 있도록 제노바 시에 넘겨졌다. 그 이후로 캐논은 제노바 시청에 보관되어 왔고, 그곳에서 전문가 팀이 그것을 관리해 오고 있다. 그들은 필요하면 그것을 수리하고 그것이 언제나 최상의 상태에 있도록 확실히 한다. (당신은 전문가가 되기 위해 악기에 대해 많은 것을 알아야 한다.) 이러한 이유로 오늘날도 그 바이올린은 Paganini 시대의 모습과 거의 똑같은 모습이다.

하지만 캐논이 항상 진열장 안에만 보관되는 것은 아니다. 그것이 시청 밖으로 나오는 특별한 행사가 있다. 2년마다 프레미오 파가니니(Premio Paganini)라고 불리는 음악 경연 대회가 제노바에서 열린다. 상으로 우승자는 Paganini의 유명한 바이올린을 하루 동안 연주하게 되는데, 이것은 대단한 영예이다.

어휘

instrument 명 도구; *악기 worth 형 ~의 가치가 있는 cannon 명 대포 talented 형 재능 있는 take care of ~을 돌보다 city hall 시청 expert 명 전문가 care for ~을 돌보다, 관리하다 repair 동 수리하다 necessary 형 필수적인 top 명 꼭대기 *형 최고의 condition 명 상태 time 명 시간; *시대 showcase 명 진열장 reward 명 보상, 상 get to-v ~하게 되다 honor 명 영예 [문제] musician 명 음악가 second-most 형 두 번째로 가장 많은

3행   It was made in 1743 by **one of** the most famous **violinmakers**, Giuseppe Guarneri.
- one of + 복수명사: ~중 하나

16행   Because of this, the violin looks almost the same today **as** it *did* in Paganini's time.
- as: ~와 같이, 마찬가지로
- did: looked를 대신하는 대동사

22행   As a reward, the winner gets to play Paganini's famous violin for one day, **which** is a great honor.
- which: 앞 절 내용 전체(As a reward ... for one day)를 선행사로 하는 계속적 용법의 관계대명사

Reading 2   p.66

②

해석

Niccolò Paganini는 1782년에 이탈리아 제노바에서 태어났다. 그는 11세에 자신의 첫 바이올린 연주회를 했고 빠르게 훌륭한 음악가로 알려지게 되었다. 그의 연주는 굉장히 놀라웠기 때문에 어떤 사람들은 Paganini가 그의 영혼을 악마에게 팔았음이 틀림없다고 생각했다. 그러나 연구가들에 의하면 Paganini는 태생적으로 타고난 예술가였다. 그는 아주 긴 손가락을 가졌는데, 이것은 그가 어려운 곡들을 쉽게 연주할 수 있게 해주었다. Paganini는 위대한 작곡가이기도 했다. 그는 자신의 공연을 위해 많은 곡을 썼다. 그의 작품들 중 일부는 지금까지 쓰인 가장 어려운 바이올린 작품에 속한다.

어휘

give a concert 연주회를 열다   soul 몡영혼   devil 몡악마   according to ~에 따르면   researcher 몡연구원 natural-born 혱타고난   composer 몡작곡가   as well (문장의 끝에서) ~도 역시   performance 몡공연   work 몡일; *작품   [문제] mysterious 혱기이한, 신비로운   talent 몡재능

구문 해설

4행   ..., some people thought Paganini **must have sold** his soul to the devil.
- must have v-ed: ~했음이 틀림없다 (과거의 일에 대한 단정적 추측)

7행   He had very long fingers, **which** *allowed him to play* difficult songs easily.
- which: very long fingers를 선행사로 하는 계속적 용법의 주격 관계대명사로, and they로 바꾸어 쓸 수 있음
- allow + 목적어 + to-v: ~가 …하게 하다

Unit Review

A [Reading 1] powerful, nicknamed, favorite, kept, winner [Reading 2] long

B **1** reward **2** performance **3** natural-born **4** honor **5** composer **6** expert

Reading 1 해석

1743년에, Giuseppe Guarneri라는 이름의 한 바이올린 제작자는 매우 강력한 소리를 내는 바이올린을 만들었다. 그것은 Niccolò Paganini라는 바이올리니스트에게 주어졌는데, 그는 그 바이올린에 '캐논'이라는 별명을 붙여줬다. 캐논은 Paganini가 가장 좋아하는 악기였고, 그가 1840년에 사망했을 때, 그것은 제노바 시에 기증되었다. 오늘날, 그 바이올린은 수백만 달러의 가치가 있고 제노바 시청의 진열장에 보관되어 있다. 2년마다, 음악 경연 대회의 행운의 우승자는 하루 동안 캐논을 연주할 수 있도록 허락된다.

Reading 2 해석

Niccolò Paganini는 뛰어난 바이올린 연주자이자 작곡가였는데, 그는 타고난 재능과 긴 손가락 때문에 어려운 곡을 쉽게 연주할 수 있었다.

UNIT 16 The Economy

Reading 1

[Before Reading] I guess it would be inconvenient if everything was made in different sizes and shapes.

1 ③ **2** ① **3** ③ **4** ① **5** improve trade and public safety **6** ④

해석

전구를 사러 상점에 갈 때 당신은 그 전구가 당신의 조명기구에 맞을 것임을 안다. 카메라 배터리를 살 때 당신은 그것이 당신의 카메라에 너무 클지 혹은 너무 작을지 걱정할 필요가 없다. 당신은 자전거 바퀴를 교체해야 할 때, 쉽게 당신의 자전거에 맞는 바퀴를 찾을 것이다. 이 모든 것들은 비록 우리가 그것들에 대해 자주 생각하지 않을지라도, 표준에 의해 가능해졌다.

1800년대에는 많은 새로운 기술들이 개발되었다. 그러나 그것들은 표준화되지 않았고 이것은 많은 문제점들을 일으켰다. 예를 들어, 초기 철로는 동일한 크기가 아니었다. (많은 사람들은 기차로 나라를 횡단하기를 희망했다.) 어떤 것들은 다른 것들보다 더 넓었다. 이것 때문에 기차들은 장거리 이동 시 어려움을 겪었다. 미국에서는 불을 끄는 데 사용되는 장비도 표준화되지 않았다. 볼티모어에서 큰 불이 났을 때, 다른 도시의 소방관들이 도우러 왔다. 그러나 그들은 볼티모어의 장비에 그들의 호스를 끼울 수가 없었다. 각 호스가 다른 크기였던 것이다!

사람들은 무역과 공공 안전을 향상시키기 위해 표준이 필요하다고 결정했다. 1947년에 국제 표준화 기구(ISO)가 창설되었다. ISO는 표준이 확실하게 지켜지도록 세계 각국과 일한다. 그러므로 다음번에 전구를 사는데 그것이 당신의 조명기구에 맞는다면 ISO에 감사하라.

light bulb 전구   fit 통(꼭) 맞다; 끼워 맞추다, 끼우다   wheel 명바퀴   standard 명표준 (standardize 통표준화하다 standardization 명표준화)   develop 통발전하다   cause 통유발하다   railroad track 철로   cross 통(길·사막 등을) 가로지르다   distance 명거리   equipment 명장비   hose 명(물을 끄는) 호스, 수도용 관   improve 통향상시키다 trade 명거래, 무역   public 형공공의, 공중의   organization 명기구, 조직

구문 해설

13행   ..., the equipment [(that was) used to fight fires] was not standardized **either**.

- either: 《부정문》 ~도 역시

19행   The ISO works with the world's countries **to *make* sure** standards are followed.

- to make: '~하기 위하여'의 의미로 목적을 나타내는 부사적 용법의 to부정사
- make sure (that): ~임을 확실히 하다, 반드시 ~하게 하다

21행   So **the next time** you buy a light bulb and it fits in your lamp, thank the ISO.

- (the) next time: 다음번에 ~할 때

Reading 2   p.70

③

해석

국제 표준화 기구는 줄여서 ISO라고 불린다. 그러나 왜 두음어의 철자가 당신이 예상한 대로 'IOS'가 아니고 'ISO'일까? 그것은 그 기구가 '국제 표준화 기구'라는 글자가 언어마다 다르다는 것을 알아냈기 때문이다. 예를 들어, 그것은 영어로는 'IOS'가 되고 프랑스어로는 'OIN (Organisation Internationale de Normalisation)'이 된다. 그래서 그 기구의 창설자들은 당신이 추측한 대로 전 세계적으로 표준이 될 만능의 이름을 고르기로 했다! 그들은 '동등한'이란 의미의 그리스 단어인 'isos'에서 따온 'ISO'를 선택했다. 그래서 당신이 어느 나라에 있든지, 그 기구의 두음어는 늘 ISO이다.

어휘

for short 줄여서   letter 명(알파벳의) 철자, 글자   acronym 명두음어 (몇 개 단어의 머리글자로 된 단어)   founder 명창설자 all-purpose 형만능의, 다목적의   equal 형동등한

구문 해설

6행   ... an all-purpose name [that would be – **you guessed it** – standard across all countries]!

- you guessed it: 삽입절로 as you guessed it의 의미

Unit Review

A   **Reading 1**   standardization, tracks, equipment, creation, size

       Reading 2   languages

B   **1** fit   **2** equipment   **3** distance   **4** Trade   **5** developed   **6** standard

Reading 2 해석

국제 표준화 기구는 'ISO'가 모든 국가와 언어에 표준이 되기를 원했기 때문에 'ISO'를 두음어로 사용할 것을 선택했다.

UNIT 17 People

Reading 1

pp.72-73

Before Reading   I usually ride my bicycle with my father every weekend.

1 ①   **2** (with others) through a computer   **3** ②   **4** ②   **5** ④   **6** ④

해석

팀 호이트에 대해 들어 본 적이 있는가? 그 팀의 멤버들은 딕 호이트와 그의 아들 릭이었다. 그들은 함께 많은 마라톤 경기와 기타 대회들에 참가했다. 놀라운 것은 현재 60대인 릭이 태어날 때부터 걷지도 말하지도 못한다는 것이다.

릭은 심각한 질병으로 인해 평생 휠체어를 타고 있다. 11세 이후로 그는 컴퓨터를 통해 다른 사람들과 의사소통을 할 수 있었다. 어느 날 그는 아버지에게 5마일 달리기에 참가하고 싶다고 말했다. 그러나 그가 어떻게 그것을 할 수 있겠는가? 딕은 아들의 꿈을 실현할 방법들을 찾아보았고 마침내 그들이 함께 경기를 뛸 수 있는 방법을 생각해 냈다. 경기 중, 딕은 달리면서 휠체어에 있는 릭을 밀어 주었다. 그들은 대부분의 다른 선수들 뒤에 처져서 (경기를) 마쳤지만, 릭은 경기 중 특별한 무언가를 느꼈다. 그는 더 이상 장애가 있는 것으로 느껴지지 않았던 것이다!

이 경험은 릭과 그의 가족 모두를 영원히 변화시켰다. 이 부자로 구성된 팀은 점점 더 자주 경기에 참가하기 시작했다. (호흡 조절이 마라톤에서 중요하다.) 비록 힘들고 어려움들로 가득 찼지만 모든 도전들은 그만한 가치가 있었다. 그보다 더 중요한 것은, 팀 호이트의 이야기는 전 세계 많은 이들을 감동하게 했고 용기를 주었으며, 장애를 가진 사람들이 보통의 삶을 살 수 있다는 것을 보여 주었다.

어휘

marathon ⑲마라톤   competition ⑲경쟁; *경기   birth ⑲출생   serious ⑱심각한   medical ⑱의학의 (medical condition 질병)   communicate ⑧의사소통하다   take part in ~에 참가하다   run ⑲달리기, 경주   look for ~을 찾다   realize ⑧*실현하다; 깨닫다   finally ⑨드디어, 마침내   think up ~을 생각해 내다   handicapped ⑱장애를 가진   controlled ⑱조절된   breathing ⑲호흡   challenge ⑲도전   worth ⑱~할 가치가 있는   touch ⑧만지다; *감동시키다   encourage ⑧격려하다, 용기를 북돋우다   disability ⑲장애 (disabled ⑱장애를 가진)   normal ⑱보통의 [문제]

beyond 젠 ~을 넘어서   passion 몡 열정   affect 통 ~에 영향을 미치다   participate in ~에 참가하다   focus on ~에 집중하다

구문 해설

3행   **What**'s surprising is that Rick, *now in his 60s*, has been unable to walk ...
　　　　　　주어　　　　　　　동사　　　　　　　　　　　　　　보어

・ What: 선행사를 포함하는 관계대명사로 '~하는 것'의 의미

・ now in his 60s: Rick에 대해 부연 설명하는 전치사구

17행   **Though (they were) hard** and full of difficulties, all the challenges have been worth it.

・ Though와 hard 사이에는 they(all the challenges) were가 생략되어 있는데, 부사절의 주어가 주절의 주어와 같고 동사가 be동사일 때는 '주어 + be동사'를 생략할 수 있음

18행   ..., the story of Team Hoyt has ⎡ touched and encouraged **many** around the world
　　　　　　　　　　　　　　　　　　　　⎢ and
　　　　　　　　　　　　　　　　　　　　⎣ shown that people with disabilities can lead ...

・ many: '많은 사람들'을 뜻하는 대명사

Reading 2   p.74

⑤

해석

다음은 팀 호이트의 멤버인 릭 호이트와의 인터뷰이다.

Q 당신이 운동선수가 될 수 있으리라고 생각해 본 적이 있나요?
A 제가 태어났을 때, 의사들이 제 부모님에게 저의 뇌를 근육들과 연결할 수 없다고 말했어요. 그들은 심지어 제 아버지에게 저의 미래에 대해 잊어버리라고 말했습니다. 그러나 저희 부모님은 제가 앞에 밝은 미래가 펼쳐져 있는 특별한 소년이라고 믿었습니다. 그들의 지원 덕분에, 저는 제가 무엇이든 할 수 있다고 생각했습니다.
Q 왜 당신과 당신 아버지는 그렇게 힘든 경기에 참가했던 건가요?
A 한 가지 이유는 우리가 그것을 굉장히 좋아했다는 것이지요! 하지만 그게 유일한 이유는 아닙니다. 우리는 우리의 성취를 통해 제가 다른 모든 사람들과 똑같다는 것을 보여 줄 수 있기를 정말로 바랐습니다.
Q 경기 중에 어려움을 겪은 적이 있나요?
A 물론 있지요. 초창기에는 어느 누구도 우리와 얘기하고 싶지 않아 했어요. 어떤 사람들은 심지어 우리가 경기에 참가하는 것을 원하지 않았고, 그들은 우리에게 상당히 냉담했습니다. 결국에 사람들은 우리가 얼마나 대단한지 그리고 제가 얼마나 많이 즐기고 있는지를 깨달았습니다.

어휘

athlete 몡 운동선수   muscle 몡 근육   ahead of ~ 앞에   achievement 몡 업적   compete 통 경쟁하다, (경기에) 참가하다   cold 혱 추운; *냉담한   towards 젠 ~을 향해

11행   Finally, people realized ┌ **how** great we were
                                       ├ and
                                       └ **how** much I was enjoying myself.

• 각각의 how가 이끄는 간접의문문은 동사 realized의 목적어 역할을 함

Unit Review
p.75

A   Reading 1   wheelchair, come true, finish, competing

B   **1** challenge   **2** realize   **3** serious   **4** passion   **5** athlete   **6** competition

Reading 1 해석

딕 호이트와 그의 아들 릭은 경기에 참가할 때 그들 자신을 팀 호이트라고 불렀다. 호이트 부자와 다른 선수들과의 주요한 차이점은 릭이 휠체어에 있다는 것이었다. 어느 날, 릭은 딕에게 (달리기) 경주에 참가하고 싶다고 말했다. 아들의 꿈을 실현하기 위해서, 딕은 휠체어에 있는 릭을 밀어주며 달렸다. 그들은 경주를 완주한 마지막 팀들 중 하나였지만, 릭은 매우 행복했다. 경주 이후, 팀 호이트는 마라톤과 다른 많은 경주에 참가하기 시작했다.

UNIT 18   *Animals*

Reading 1
pp.76-77

Before Reading   I once saw a chimpanzee use a stick and a rock to eat fruit on YouTube.

1 ①   **2** ④   **3** ④   **4** to keep plastic dust out of their throats   **5** ③   **6** ②

해석

많은 사람들은 인간만이 도구를 사용한다고 생각한다. 그러나 일부 동물들은 그들의 환경에 있는 사물들을 도구로 사용한다. 예를 들어, 해달은 돌을 도구로 사용한다. 해달은 맛있는 바다 생물이 들어 있는 딱딱한 조개껍데기를 발견하면, 커다란 돌을 찾는다. 그런 다음 해달은 그 딱딱한 조개껍데기를 돌 위에 친다. 껍데기가 열리고, 해달은 안에 있는 생물을 먹는다.

침팬지 또한 도구를 사용한다. 그들은 흰개미를 잡기 위해 막대기를 사용한다. 흰개미는 흙더미 속에서 살기 때문에, 침팬지가 손으로 그것들을 잡을 수가 없다. 그래서 침팬지는 나뭇가지를 찾아서 그것의 잎들과 잔가지들을 뜯어낸다. 그리고 침팬지는 그 막대기를 완벽한 크기로 부러뜨린다. 그런 다음 침팬지는 그것(막대기)을 흰개미의 흙더미에 있는 구멍으로 조심스럽게 집어넣는다. 침팬지가 그 나뭇가지를 다시 끄집어냈을 때, 그것은 그것에 붙어 있는 맛있는 흰개미들을 즐길 수 있다.

과학자들은 동물들이 어떻게 도구를 사용하는지에 대해 더 많이 알고 싶었다. 그래서 그들은 플라스틱 관에 벌거숭이두더지쥐들을 집어넣었다. 벌거숭이두더지쥐들은 밖으로 나오기 위해 플라스틱을 씹어서 구멍을 만들었다. 흥미롭게도 그들은 씹기 전에 작은 나뭇

조각들을 앞니 뒤에 두었다. 이 '먼지 마스크'는 플라스틱 먼지가 그들의 목구멍 안으로 넘어가지 않게 해주었다. 어떻게 그런 창의성이 가능할까? 그것은 지능일까, 아니면 본능일까? 과학자들은 언젠가는 그 답을 찾기를 희망한다.

어휘

tool 圐도구   object 圐물건, 물체   sea otter 해달   shell 圐(조개 등의) 껍데기   tasty 圂맛있는   creature 圐생물   chimpanzee 圐침팬지 (= chimp)   stick 圐막대기 圂(to) ～에 달라붙다   termite 圐흰개미   mound 圐흙더미   branch 圐나뭇가지   naked mole-rat 벌거숭이두더지쥐   tube 圐관   chew 圂*(상처·구멍을) 씹어서 만들다, 씹다   get out 탈출하다, 도망치다   place 圂위치시키다, 두다   dust 圐티끌, 먼지   intelligence 圐지능   instinct 圐본능   [문제] behavior 圐행동   shellfish 圐조개   throw 圂던지다   question 圂질문하다; *이의를 제기하다

구문 해설

3행   When a sea otter finds a hard shell **with a tasty sea creature inside**, it looks for a big rock.
   • with + 명사 + 장소 부사: ～이 …에 있는 상태로[인]

12행   When the chimp pulls the branch back out, **it** can enjoy the tasty termites [that stick to *it*].

   • 첫 번째 it은 the chimp를, 두 번째 it은 the branch를 가리킴

Reading 2   p.78

②

해석

어떤 동물이 진정한 발명가인지 아닌지를 우리가 어떻게 알 수 있을까? 어떻게 우리가 그들의 행동을 설명할 수 있을까? 우리가 그들에게 물어볼 수 없기 때문에 과학자들은 그들을 관찰함으로써 이 질문에 답하고자 노력한다. 만일 도구의 사용이 타고난 능력이라면, 예를 들어, 대부분의 침팬지들은 똑같은 방식으로 막대기를 사용할 것이다. 그러나 각 침팬지는 도구를 다르게 만들고 사용한다. 게다가 어린 침팬지는 더 나이 든 침팬지를 관찰함으로써 그들의 기술을 배운다. 그들은 처음 몇 번 동안은 도구를 잘 만들지 못한다. 그러나 어린 침팬지들은 자라면서 도구 만드는 일에 더 능숙해진다. 이 모든 사실들은 우리에게 일부 동물들은 발명의 재능을 갖고 있음을 보여준다.

어휘

inventor 圐발명가 (invention 圐발명품   inventive 圂발명의 재능이 있는)   inborn 圂타고난   ability 圐능력, 재능   fact 圐사실   [문제] observer 圐관찰자

구문 해설

1행   How can we know **if** some animals are true inventors **or not**?
   • if ～ (or not): '～인지 아닌지'의 의미로, 목적어로 쓰인 명사절의 if는 whether와 바꾸어 쓸 수 있음

Unit Review

A Reading 1 tools, open, protect, intelligence

B 1 sticking 2 inborn 3 tool 4 inventor 5 behavior 6 chew

Reading 1 해석

인간은 도구를 사용하는 유일한 존재가 아니다. 일부 동물들도 그들 자신만의 도구들을 만든다. 예를 들어, 해달은 조개껍데기 안에 있는 것을 먹기 위해 바위를 이용해서 조개껍데기를 연다. 침팬지는 나뭇가지를 흰개미 굴에 넣어 그 위에 있는 흰개미들을 먹는다. 그리고 벌거숭이두더지쥐는 작은 나뭇조각들을 사용하여 그들의 목구멍을 먼지로부터 보호하는 방법을 알고 있다. 과학자들은 이러한 유형의 행동이 본능에 의한 것인지 혹은 지능에 의한 것인지를 확신하지 못하지만, 그들은 알아내고 싶어 한다.

UNIT 19 History

Reading 1

Before Reading I think it's because people sometimes do not understand the culture or language of other races.

1 ④ 2 ③ 3 They had to sit at the back of the bus. 4 ④ 5 ① 6 ④

해석

그날은 1955년 12월 1일이었다. 흑인인 로자 파크스가 앨라배마주 몽고메리의 시내버스에 올라탔고, 맨 앞 좌석에 앉았다. 버스에 있는 모든 사람들이 놀랐다. 당시 앨라배마주에서는 흑인들은 버스의 뒤쪽에 앉아야 했다. (대부분의 사람들은 자신의 자동차를 몰기보다는 버스를 타곤 했다.) 앞 좌석들은 백인들만을 위한 것이었다. 버스 기사는 화가 나서 파크스에게 (그녀의) 자리를 내주라고 말했지만, 그녀는 거부했다. 그녀는 모든 인종의 사람들은 똑같은 권리를 가져야 한다고 믿었다. 이 행동은 로자 파크스를 '현대 인권 운동의 어머니'로 바꿔 놓았다.

파크스는 경찰에 붙잡혔고 투옥되었다. 그녀의 재판은 일 년이 넘도록 계속되었다. 재판 기간 동안 몽고메리에 있는 대부분의 흑인들은 시내버스를 타지 않았다. 그것은 항의였다. 버스 좌석에 대한 규정들 외에도, 그들은 앨라배마주의 다른 많은 불공평한 법규들에 대해서도 항의하고 있었다. 예를 들어, 흑인 아이들은 스쿨버스를 타는 것이 허용되지 않았다.

마침내 재판이 끝났다. 미국 대법원은 시내버스에 백인과 흑인을 대상으로 분리된 좌석을 두는 것이 불공평하다고 결정했다. 그것은 인권 운동을 위한 중요한 승리였고, 이는 로자 파크스 덕분이었다.

어휘

take a seat 앉다 (seat 명 좌석, 자리) give up ~을 포기하다[내주다] refuse 동 거부하다 race 명 인종 right 명 권리
turn A into B A를 B로 바꾸다 jail 명 감옥, 교도소 trial 명 재판 last 동 지속되다, 계속하다 protest 명 동 항의(하다)

unfair ⓗ불공평한　law ⓜ법, 법규　allow ⓥ허용하다　Supreme Court 대법원　separate *ⓗ분리된 ⓥ분리시키다
victory ⓜ승리　civil rights 인권, 시민권　movement ⓜ움직임; *(정치·사회적) 운동　[문제] society ⓜ사회; *협회
modern-day ⓗ현대의　stand up for ～을 변호[옹호]하다　equal ⓗ동등한　ordinary ⓗ보통의, 평범한

구문 해설

15행　For example, black children **were not allowed to ride** on school buses.
- be not allowed to-v: ～하는 것이 금지되어 있다, 허용되지 않다

17행　The US Supreme Court decided (that) **it** was unfair **to have** separate seats for whites and blacks on city buses.
- it은 가주어, to have 이하는 진주어임

Reading 2　　　　　　　　　　　　　　　　　　　　　　　　　　　　　　　　　　　　　p.82

⑤

해석

　1876년에서 1965년까지 미국의 일부 지역에는 공공장소에서 백인을 유색인들과 분리해두는 법규들이 있었다. 이것들은 짐 크로 법(Jim Crow laws)이라고 알려져 있었다. 이 법규들 때문에 많은 학교와 식당, 극장, 그리고 호텔에는 '백인 전용' 표지판이 있었다. 백인이 아닌 사람들이 사용할 수 있었던 장소들은 '유색인'이라는 표지판으로 표시되었다. 일부 기차와 버스의 좌석들도 인종에 따라 분리되어 있었다. 심지어 많은 주에서는 백인과 유색인 간의 결혼도 금지되어 있었다. 다행히 이러한 법규들은 1964년의 공민권법에 의해 마침내 종결되었다.

어휘

sign ⓜ표시, 표지판　non-white ⓜ백인이 아닌 사람, 유색인　mark ⓥ표시하다　colored ⓗ유색인의　divide ⓥ나누다
marriage ⓜ결혼　fortunately ⓟ다행히　[문제] private ⓗ사적인, 사유의　community ⓜ지역 사회　regardless
of ～에 관계없이

구문 해설

1행　... laws in some parts of America [**to** ***keep*** *white people separated* from ... places].
- to keep: laws를 수식하는 형용사적 용법의 to부정사
- keep + 목적어 + v-ed: ～을 …되게 두다

Unit Review　　　　　　　　　　　　　　　　　　　　　　　　　　　　　　　　　　p.83

A　Reading 1　white, protest, ride, separate　Reading 2　laws

B　**1** allow　**2** law　**3** trial　**4** protest　**5** separate　**6** mark

공민권법이 제정되기 전까지, 많은 미국 주들에는 백인과 유색인을 분리해두는 <u>법규들</u>이 있었다.

UNIT 20 Mysteries

Reading 1

pp.84-85

Before Reading I truly believe strange things exist, such as aliens and UFOs!

1 ③   **2** ④   **3** ①, ④   **4** ③   **5** ③   **6** ④

해석

나스카 라인은 페루의 나스카 사막에 있는 일련의 거대한 그림들이다. 그것들은 기원전 200년과 기원후 600년 사이에 그려진 것이라고 여겨진다. 그 선들은 새, 거미, 원숭이, 그리고 기하학적인 모양들과 같은 300개의 형상을 포함한다. 그 그림들은 너무 커서 오직 하늘에서만 선명하게 보일 수 있다. 그러므로, 고대 사람들이 비행 기술도 없이 이 형상들을 땅에 그릴 수 있었다는 것은 놀랍다. 게다가, 이 그림들이 수천 년 동안 지속되어 왔다는 것은 믿기 힘들다.

1920년대 그것들의 발견 이후로 사람들은 이 선들이 무엇을 위해 그려진 것인지를 알아내기 위해 노력해왔다. 어떤 사람들은 그 선들이 종교적 이유로 만들어졌다고 제안한다. 그 선들과 모양들은 나스카인들이 숭배했던 신들을 위해 만들어졌을지도 모른다. 커다란 그림들을 만듦으로써, 나스카 사람들은 하늘에 있는 신들이 그 형상들을 볼 수 있기를 희망했다. 반면에 어떤 사람들은 그 선들은 거대한 달력이었다고 말한다. <u>그들은 그 형상들이 별과 계절의 변화와 연관되어 있다고 믿는다.</u> 어떤 사람들은 심지어 그 선들이 우주선의 활주로로서 외계인들에 의해 그려진 것이라고 제안하기도 한다. 그러나 이것들 중 어느 것도 그 선들을 명확히 설명할 수 없는 것 같다. 수천 년이 지난 후에도 이 중요한 예술작품은 여전히 불가사의이다.

어휘

Nazca 몡나스카 (Nazcan 혱나스카(인)의)   a series of 일련의   giant 혱거대한   drawing 몡그림 (draw 동그리다) figure 몡*형상; 숫자   ancient 혱고대의   discovery 몡발견   suggest 동제안하다   religious 혱종교적인   worship 동숭배하다   calendar 몡달력   alien 몡외계인   runway 몡활주로   spaceship 몡우주선   artwork 몡예술작품 [문제] artistic 혱예술의   Peruvian 혱페루의   puzzling 혱당혹케 하는, 헷갈리게 하는   be related to ~에 관련되어 있다

구문 해설

2행   **It is believed that** they were drawn between 200 BC and 600 AD.
- it is believed that ~: ~이라고 여겨지다 (it은 가주어, that 이하는 진주어)

10행   **Since** their discovery in the 1920s, people *have tried* to find out <u>what these lines were drawn for</u>.
- since: ~ 이후로

- have tried: 계속의 현재완료 시제로 '~해 오고 있다'의 의미
- what these lines were drawn for: find out의 목적어로 쓰인 간접의문문 (what ... for는 '무엇 때문에', '왜 (why)'의 의미)

12행   The lines and shapes **may have been** made for <u>the gods</u> [(that) the Nazcans worshipped].

- may have v-ed: ~했을지도 모른다 (과거 사실의 불확실한 추측)

Reading 2   p.86

③

해석

Maria Reiche는 자신의 삶을 놀라운 나스카 라인을 연구하는 데 보낸 고고학자였다. 그녀는 비록 독일에서 태어났지만 대부분의 삶을 페루에서 살았다. 그곳에서 그녀는 나스카 라인을 볼 기회가 있었고 그것들에 큰 관심을 갖게 되었다. 약 40년간, Maria는 그 경이로운 나스카 라인을 연구했고 그것들을 보호하기 위해 노력했다. 불행히도, 페루 사람들은 유산으로서 그것들의 중요성을 알지 못했다. 페루 정부는 심지어 그 그림들 중 하나를 가로지르는 고속도로를 건설하였다! (이 고속도로는 팬아메리칸 하이웨이의 일부이며, 그것은 남미에 있는 대부분의 국가를 연결한다.) 마침내 Maria는 사람들이 그것들을 손상시키는 것을 막도록 페루 정부를 설득했다. 그녀의 노력 덕분에 유네스코는 1994년에 나스카 라인을 세계문화유산으로 선포했다.

어휘

archaeologist ⑲고고학자   unfortunately ⑭안타깝게도   be aware of ~을 알다   heritage ⑲유산, 상속 재산
highway ⑲고속도로   persuade ⑧(~하라고) 설득하다   effort ⑲노력   declare ⑧선언하다

구문 해설

1행   Maria Reiche was <u>an archaeologist</u> [who **spent her life studying** ... Nazca Lines].

- spend + 시간 + v-ing: ~ 하면서 (시간)을 보내다

Unit Review   p.87

A   Reading 1   religious, calendar, spaceships, mystery   Reading 2   archaeologist
B   **1** religious   **2** effort   **3** discovery   **4** worship   **5** figures   **6** persuade

Reading 2 해석

Maria Reiche는 페루에서 나스카 라인을 연구하고 보호했던 독일의 <u>고고학자</u>였고, 그녀의 노력은 1994년 그것이 세계문화유산이 되도록 도왔다.

MEMO

MEMO

MEMO

MEMO

MEMO

JUNIOR
READING EXPERT

Level 3